Design Ideas and Accessories

Ritu bhargav

Design Ideas and Accessories

First Edition: 2005

© Copyright with the author

No part of this book may be reproduced, stored in a retrieval system or transmitted, in any form or by any means, mechanical, photocopying, recording or otherwise, without any prior written permission of the publisher.

Price Rs. 499/-

Published by Kuldeep Jain

an imprint of

B. Jain Publishers (P) Ltd.
1921, Street No. 10, Chuna Mandi,
Paharganj, New Delhi - 110 055 (INDIA)
Phones: 2358 100, 2358 1300, 2358 0800
Fax: 011-2358 0471; Email: bjain@vsnl.com
Website: www.bjainbooks.com

Printed in India by

Brijbasi Art Press Ltd.
E-46/11, Okhla Industrial Area, Phase-II, New Delhi-110020
Phones: 26386232, 26387451 Fax: 26383766

ISBN: 81-8056-528-9
BOOK CODE: BB-5784

Acknowledgement

I dedicate this book to my parents and my mentor Daisaku Ikeda. I thank the publisher, Mr. Kuldeep for giving me the opportunity to produce this book.

I would like to thank the professional contributor Sanjeev Das and Nidhi Sansi for helping me in Illustrations and Mr. M. S. Rawat of Designers Group. Without their support the completion of this project would not have been possible.

On a personal note I would like to deeply thank my husband, Ashwin for his constant support and patience and also my in-laws for helping to look after Avi and Aayush while I was working for the drawings and text. I would also like to thank my brother Sunjey and my sister Sangeeta for their constant encouragement. All of them have been a driving force for me.

Preface

In today's fashion world, designers sketch their creative designs & inspirations on paper before putting across the final product or garment. Not only colors but also all the cuts, stitches, embellishments, accessories such as bags, shoes etc. are also represented in the sketch before they are put on or with a garment.

This book accomplishes the needs of students & artists who are pursuing or want to pursue fashion designing. This book comprises of the different design ideas starting with necklines, collars to various accessories like bags & shoes. A special unit on object drawing is also a part of this book.

Similar to our previous series this book gives a good collection of sketches of necklines, collars, yokes, tucks, skirts, trousers etc. along with those, which are currently in fashion. This helps us in knowing the fashion world better and faster. This book provides an added knowledge to the previous series, which talks about basic sketching & rendering.

The book is in a simplified form of all other books for helping in better understanding of fashion illustration by the students & emphasizing the minute details in the garment.

SELF EMPOWERING PRAYER
TO BECOME A MAN/WOMAN OF UNLIMITED SELF-ESTEEM

- To believe in the greatness of my life.

- My mission is to be happy-not to master suffering.

- I value my own life.

- I appreciate my own life and that has nothing to do with someone else validating me.

- I have to have the most reverence for my life.

- I appreciate my flaws, my accomplishments, my defeats, my losses, my victories, all that I have created. I truly APPRECIATE MY TALENT. I really appreciate everything about my life: all the things about me, that make me incredibly unique and wonderful.

- I seel the miracle of my own life.

- The results we see in our lives are a reflection of our life condition.

- Every one of my wildest dreams will be fulfilled beyond my wildest imagination.

- I trust my life. The billion dollar check I am afraid to cash does exist.

- I have EVERYTHING I need for my happiness.

- Empower the good and make evil people powerless and lead them to the path of good.

CONTENTS

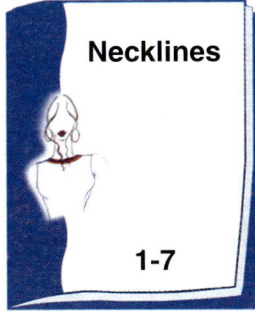 **Necklines** 1-7	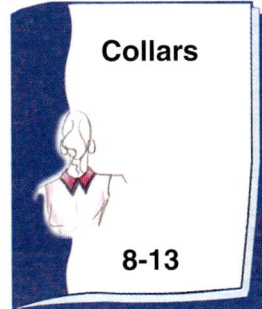 **Collars** 8-13	 **Sleeves** 14-18	 **Skirt** 19-31
 **Tops** 32-42	 **Pants** 43-50	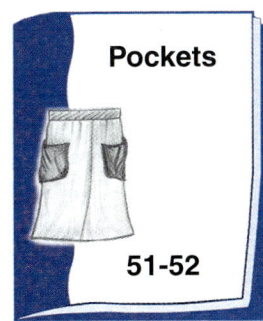 **Pockets** 51-52	 **Tucks** 53
 **Yokes** 54	 **Shirring** 55	 **Frills & Flounces** 56-57	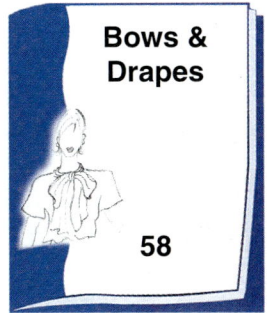 **Bows & Drapes** 58
 **Jabot & Quilting** 59	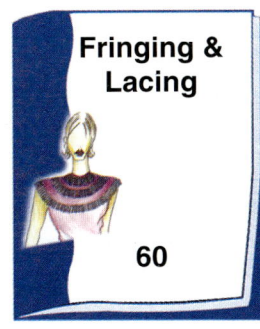 **Fringing & Lacing** 60	 **Kids Wear** 61-66	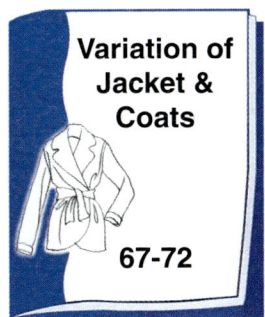 **Variation of Jacket & Coats** 67-72

One Piece Dress  73-84	**Frocks**  85-91	**Jumpsuit**  92-94	**Poncho** 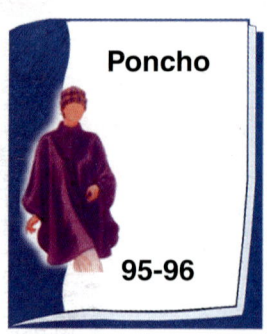 95-96
Dress  97-107	**Jacket**  108-109	**Nightwear** 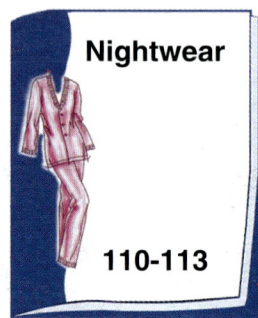 110-113	**Loungewear**  114-120
Nature Study  121	**Object Drawing** 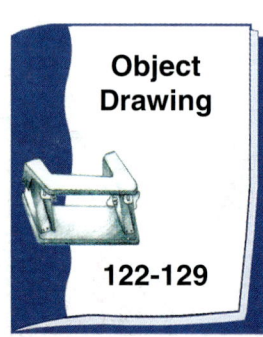 122-129	**Shoes**  130-132	**Bags**  133-137
Neck Accessories 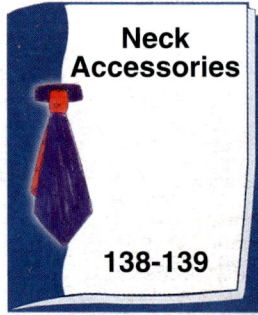 138-139	**Belts** 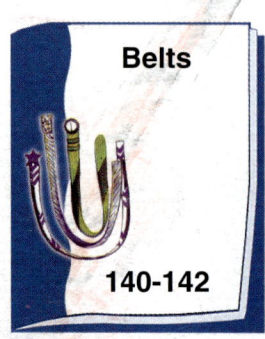 140-142	**Composition** 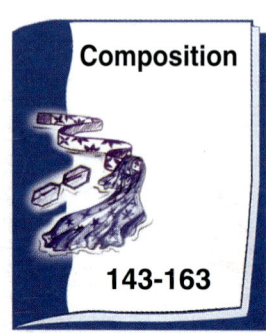 143-163	**Hats** 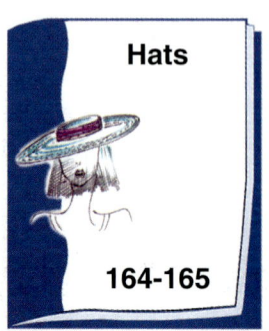 164-165

Necklines

NECKLINES
Neckline shapes have many variations with a selection of collars and trimmings from which to choose.

Jewel
It gives the illusion of roundness and eye travel in very small area.

Round
It gives rounded look and it is not suitable for heavy and broad figure.

U-Shaped
It adds length to the neck and depth also. In this, eyes appear to move away from the face. It is more suitable for person with round face.

Square
It gives the illusion of angular look and is not suitable for a person with a square face.

Necklines

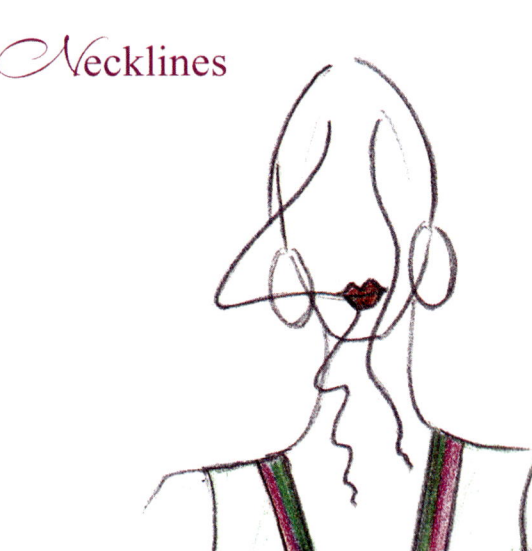

Glass — It has the same effect as the square neckline has but the effect is softer

V-Shaped — It gives a look of slenderness

Sweet-Heart — It gives a very soft and feminine look.

Sweet-Heart

Necklines

Matka

Matka

Funnel

A high neckline that extends up the neck.

Scalloped

A decoratively edged neckline that would be faced.

Necklines

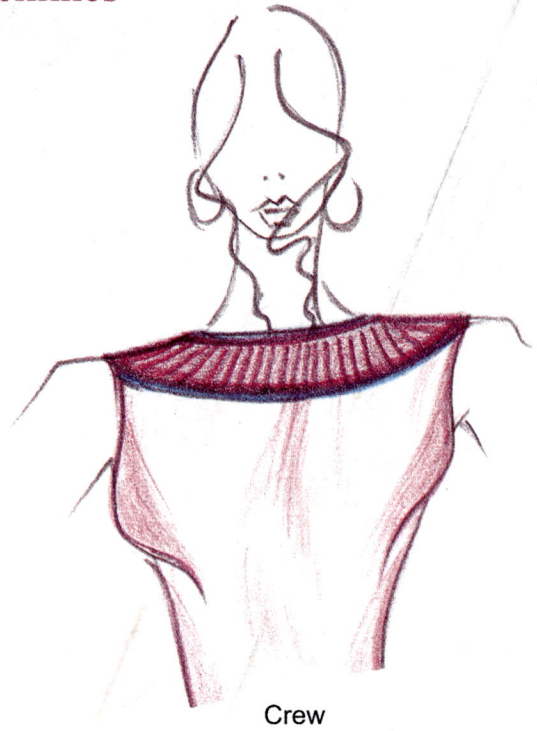

Crew

A snug-fitting neckline trimmed with a knitted rib as in tee shirts and sweatshirts.

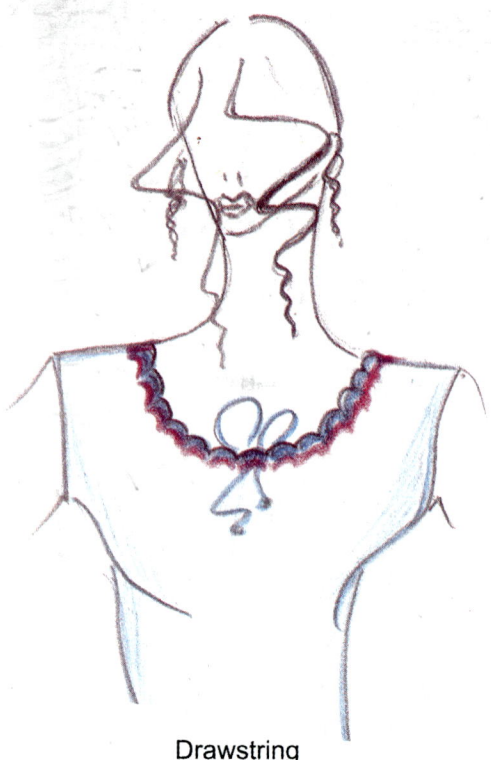

Drawstring

As the elasticised neckline but here controlled with an adjustable drawstring.

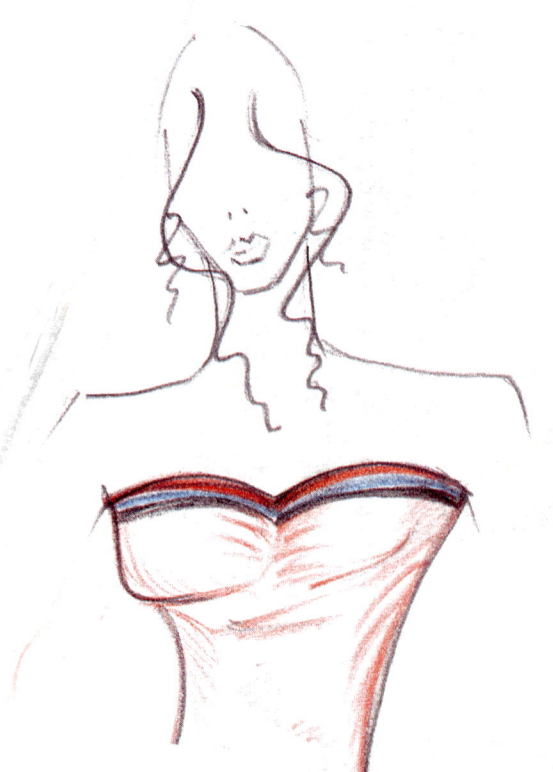

Tanktube

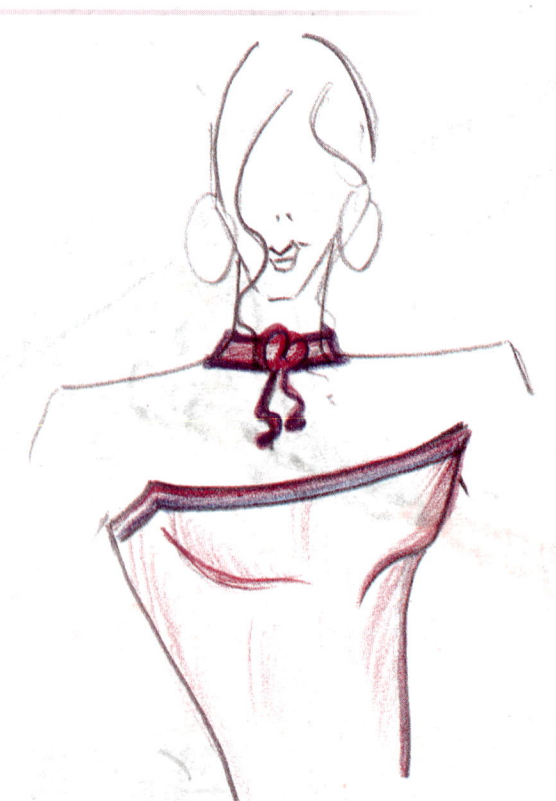

Halter-Back

The bodice of a garment is extended round the neck to form straps and a fastening. There is usually only a band of fabric across the back. a band of fabric across the back.

Necklines

A jewel neckline with a slit at the front or the back which is faced and fastened, edge, at the neck with a single button and loop.

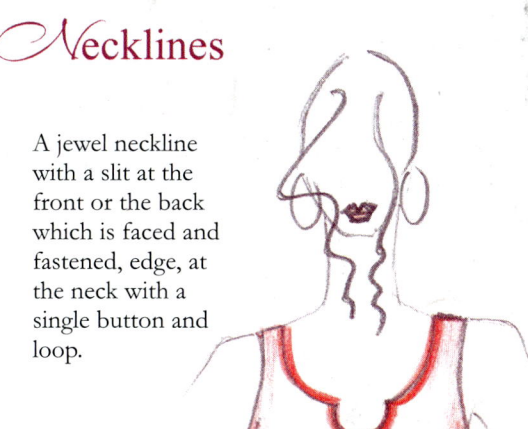

Keyhole

Keyhole

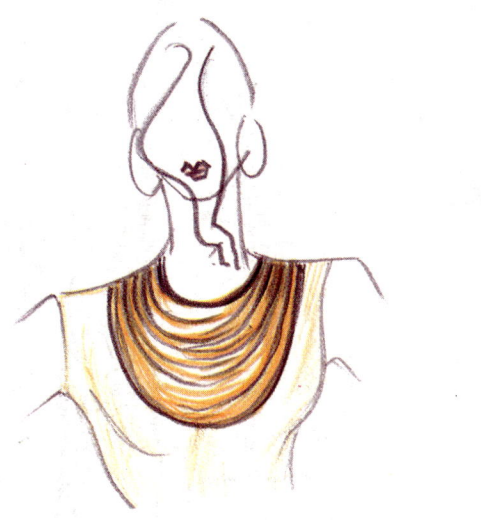

Cowl
A draped neckline, usually cut in bias to create more soft folds of draping.

Necklines

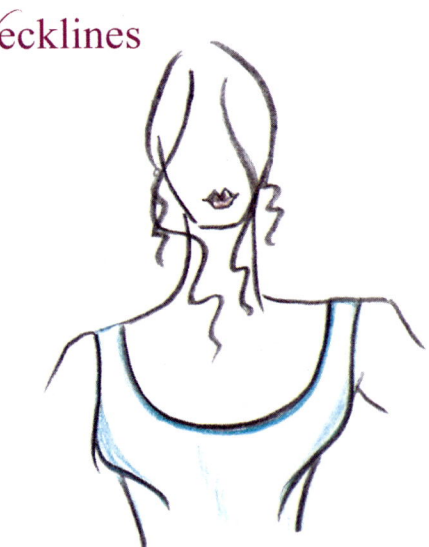

Scoop

A shallow but wide neckline.

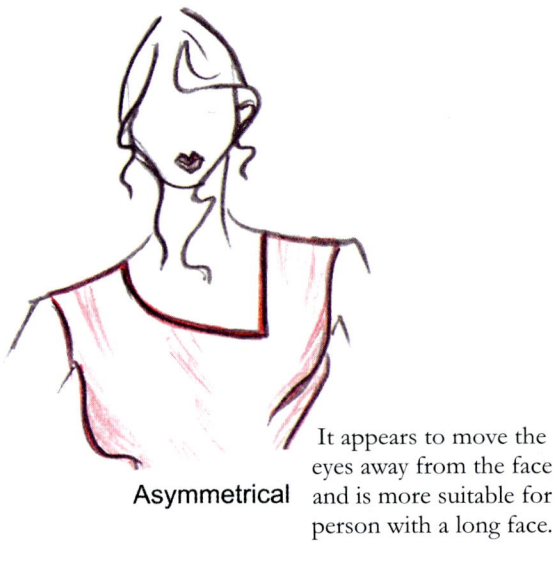

Asymmetrical

It appears to move the eyes away from the face and is more suitable for person with a long face.

Asymmetrical

Necklines

Variations of Necklines

Collars

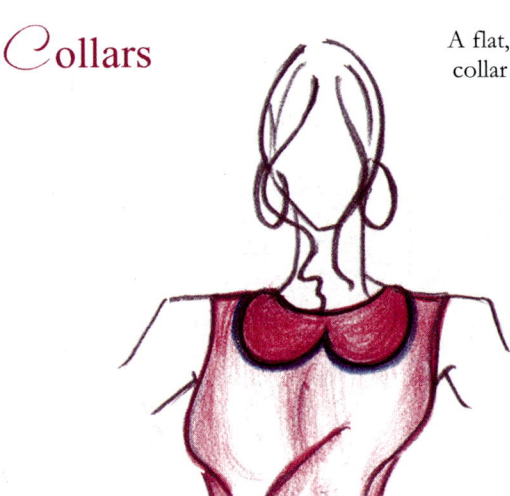

A flat, curved shaped collar with no stand.

One-piece peter pan

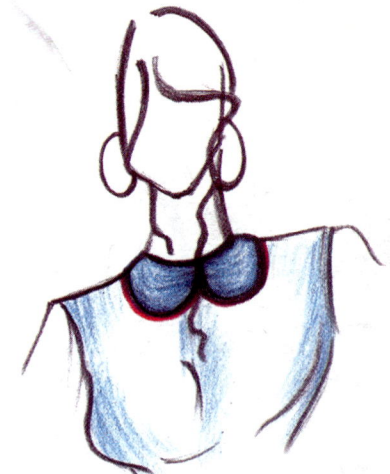

2 piece peter pan

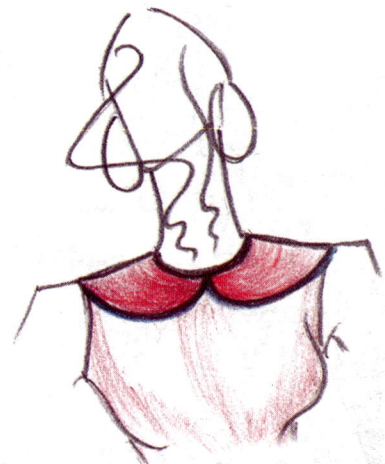

1 piece cape pan

It adds more roundness and width; the collar is emphasized.

A V-shaped neck with a straight collar set in that meets at the front.

Chelsea

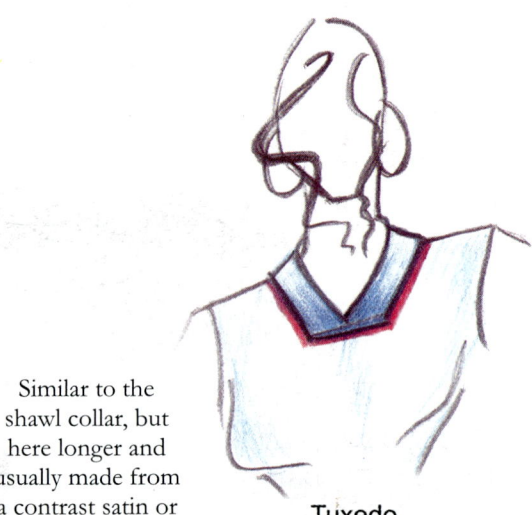

Similar to the shawl collar, but here longer and usually made from a contrast satin or silk for use on evening wear.

Tuxedo

Sailor's

A v-shaped neckline with a collar similar to the Chelsea but with deep, cape-like, square back, usually trimmed with contrasting braid.

Collars

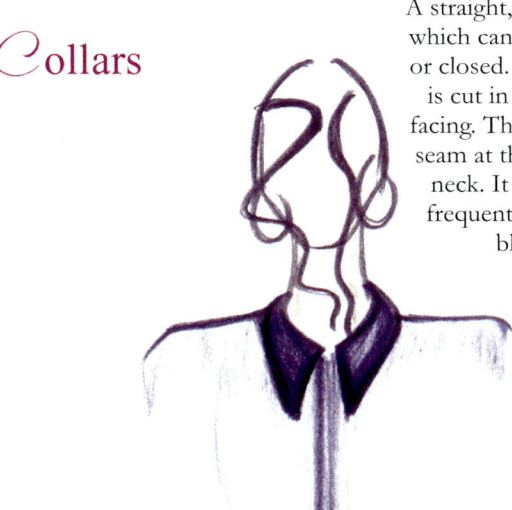

A straight, pointed collar, which can be worn open or closed. The top collar is cut in one with the facing. There is only one seam at the back of the neck. It is seen most frequently on shirt or blouses.

Convertible shirt (open)

As the shawl collar but here with a notch cut out to create shaping.

Notched Shawl

Convertible shirt (close)

Bishop: A Shirt-type collar with points extending into cap shapes & no fastening down the front.

Bishop

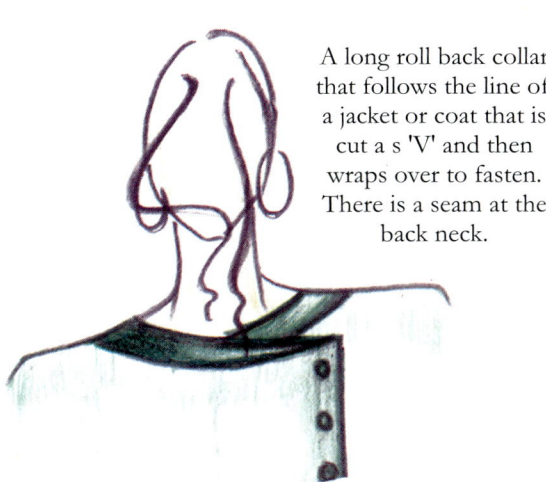

A long roll back collar that follows the line of a jacket or coat that is cut a s 'V' and then wraps over to fasten. There is a seam at the back neck.

Shawl

Chinese

Collars

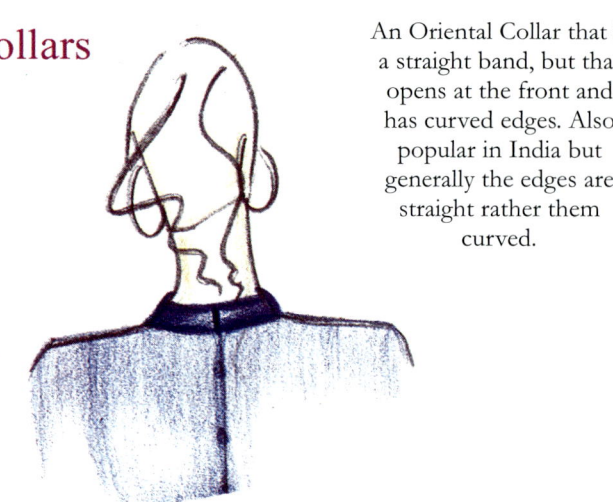

An Oriental Collar that is a straight band, but that opens at the front and has curved edges. Also popular in India but generally the edges are straight rather them curved.

Nehru

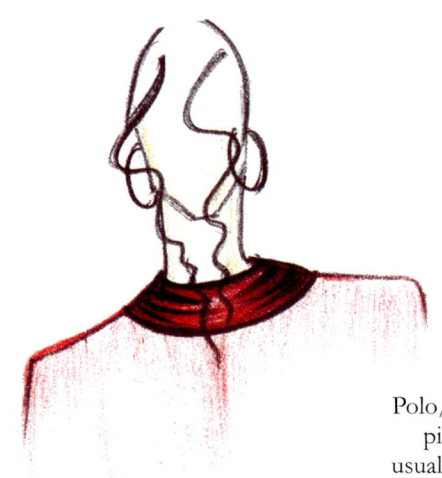

Polo/Turtle : A wide piece of fabric usually knitted or cut on the cross, that folds back to form a roll neck collar.

Polo/Turtle

Bow-Tie

Bow Tie: Tied in a soft bow

Bertha

Bertha : A cape line collar that usually covered the shoulders. It was generally made from lace & was popular in the nineteenth & only twentieth centuries.

Collars

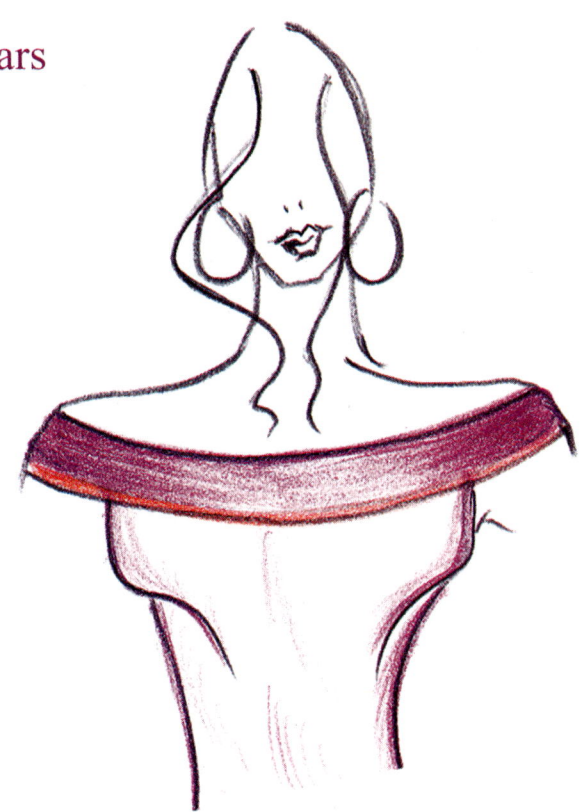

A feminine neckline where the shoulders are bared revealing the whole neck.

Off-shoulder

Angrakha Collar

Collars

Variation of Collars

Collars

Variation of Collars

Sleeves

Plain Sleeve

Bush

Puff

Hankerchief

Hankerchief with Gathers

Bell

Sleeves

Shirt

Leg-o-Mutton

Ruffle

Coat

Juliet

Kurta

Sleeves

Flared

Petal

Half Cap

Full Cap

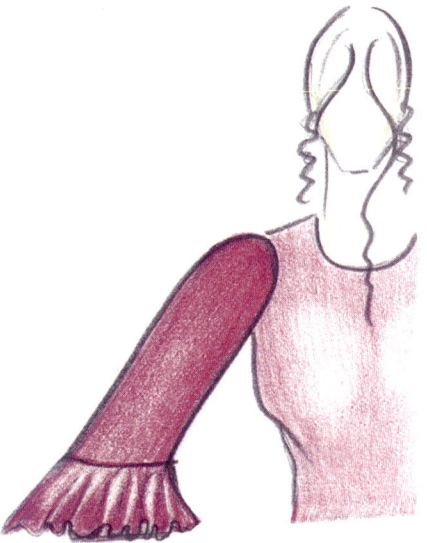
Plounce

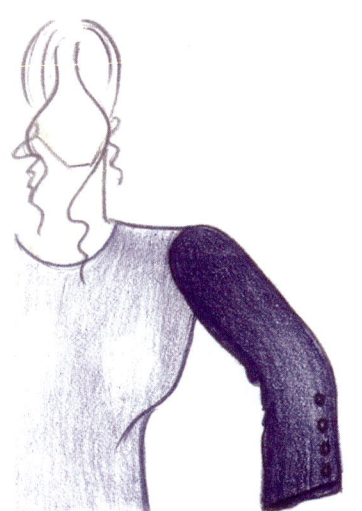
Wedding

Sleeves

Kimono

Dolman

Virego

Sleeves

Variation of Sleeves

18

Skirt

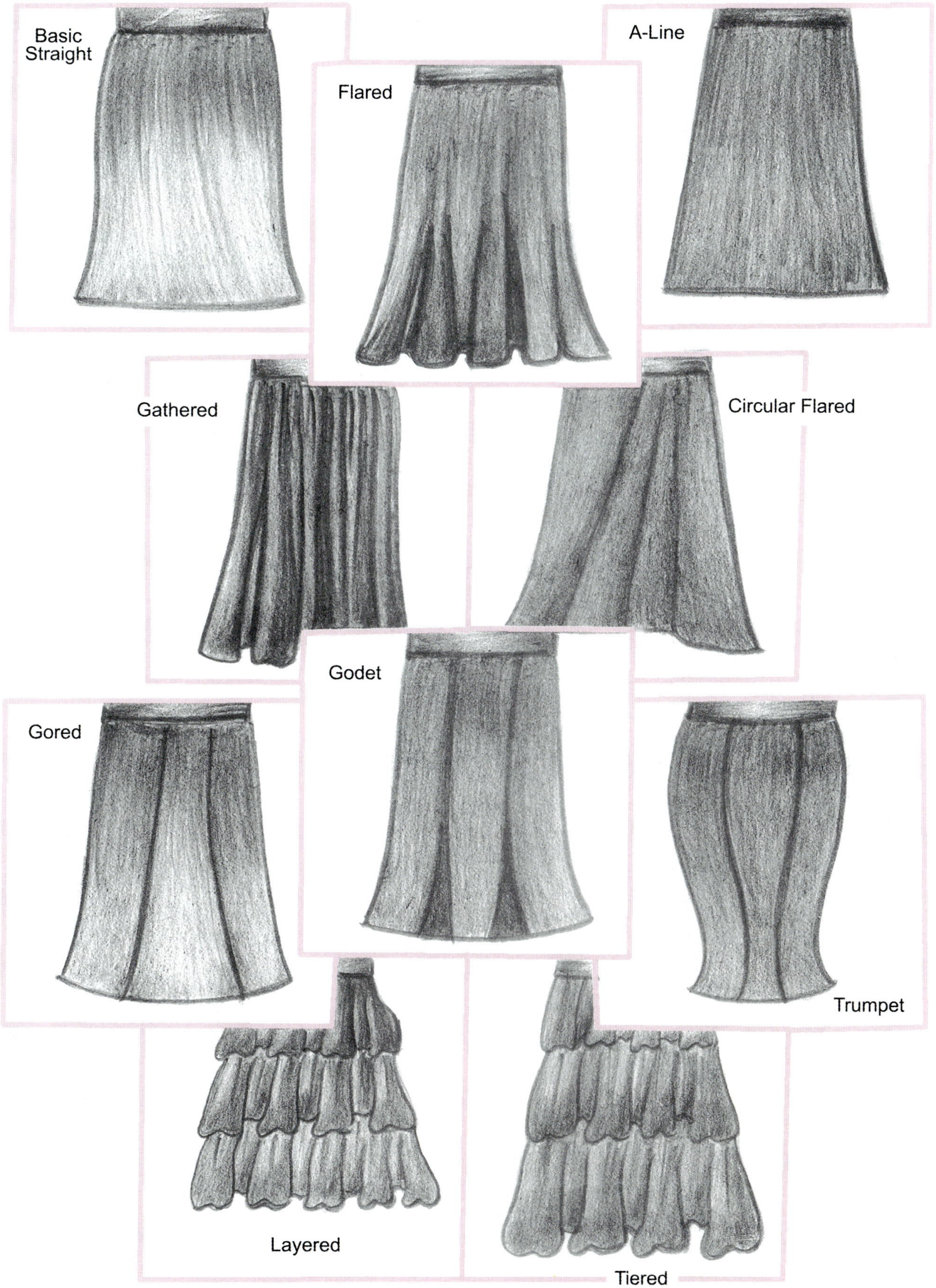

- Basic Straight
- Flared
- A-Line
- Gathered
- Circular Flared
- Gored
- Godet
- Trumpet
- Layered
- Tiered

Skirt

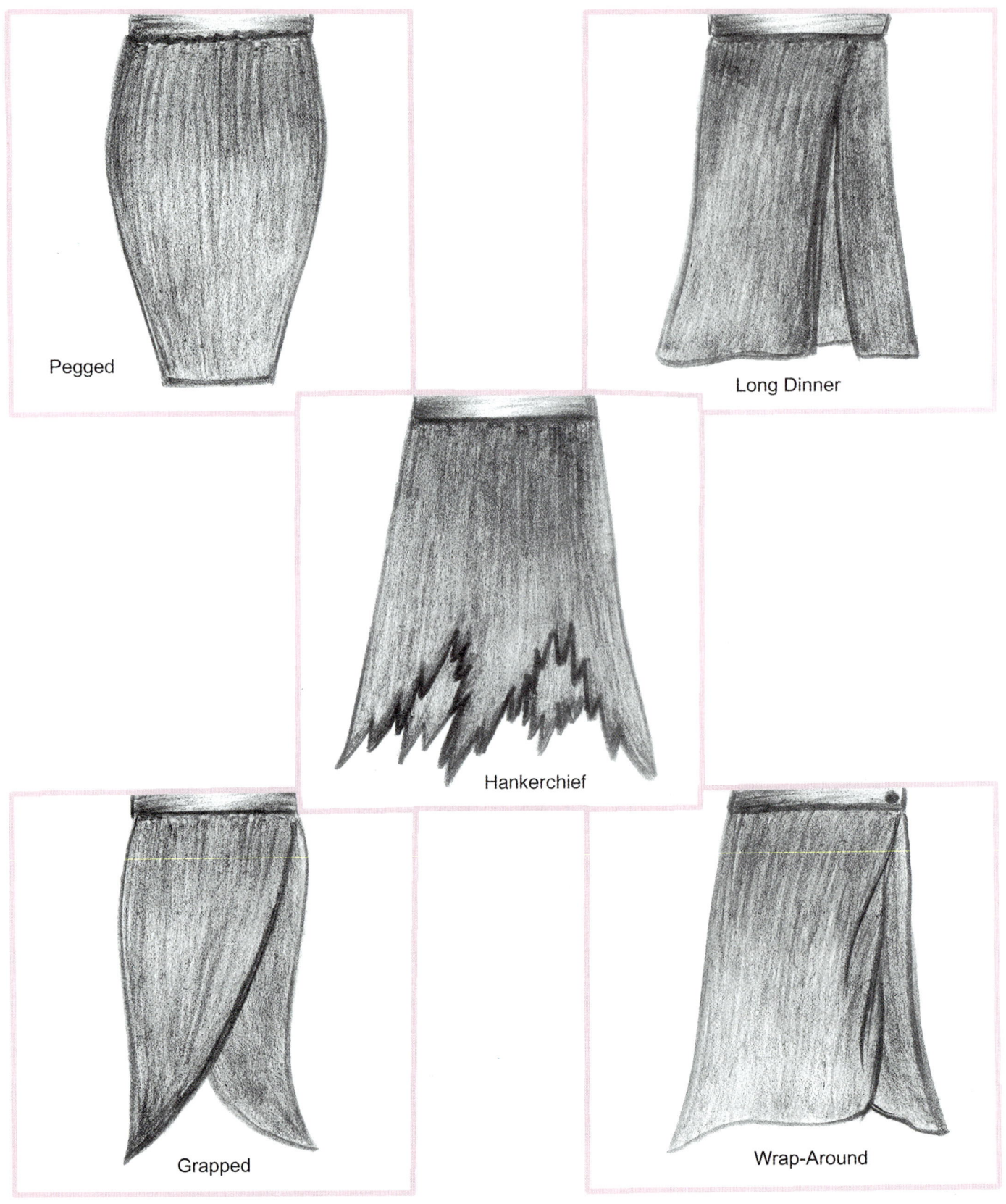

Skirt

- Circular
- Gored & Hared 
- Bubble
- A-Line
- Mini 
- Drape & Wrapover 
- Trumpet 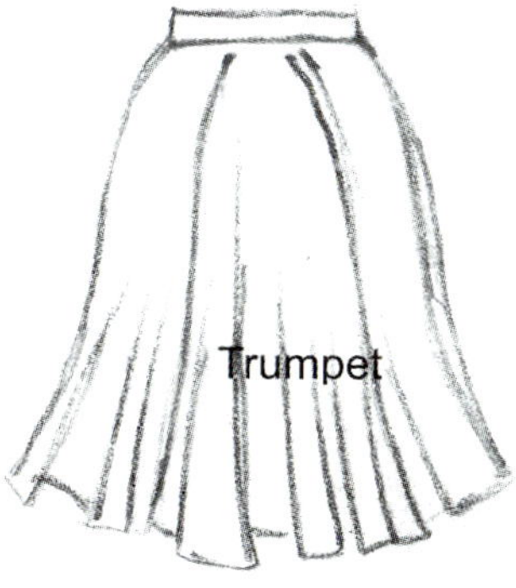
- Pelat
- Wrap-Around  
- Long Dinner Skirt
- Tennis

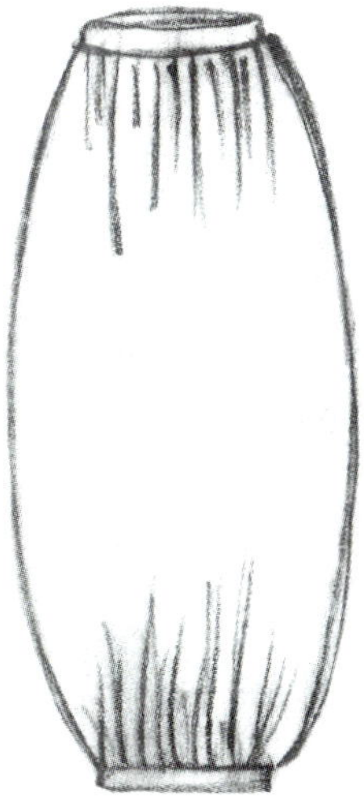

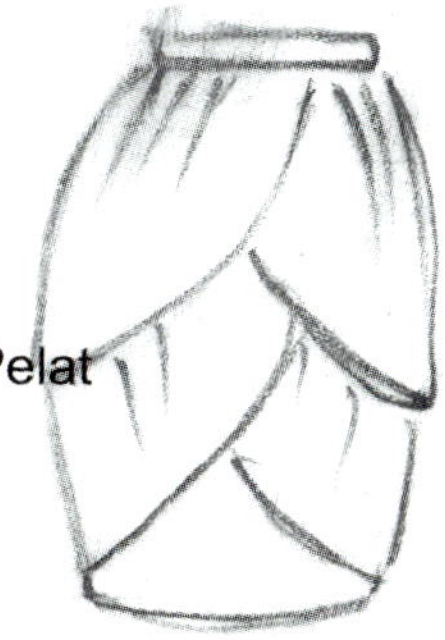

# Skirt

Variation of Skirts

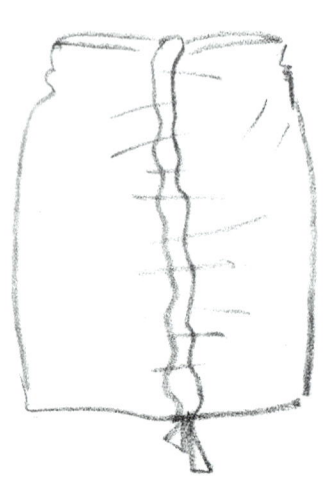

Variation of Skirts

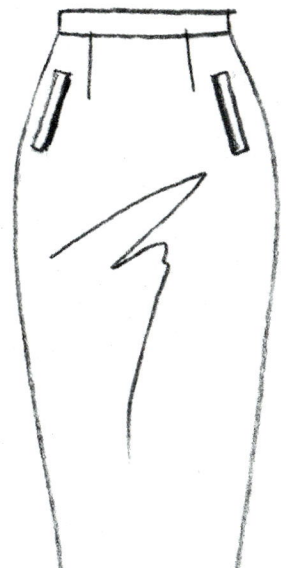

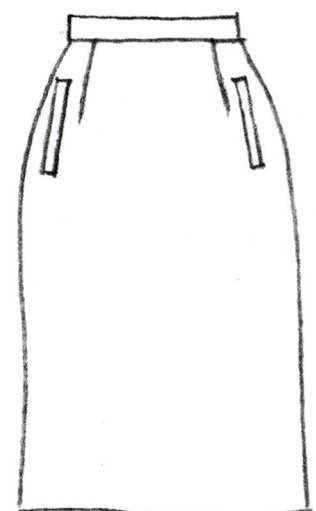
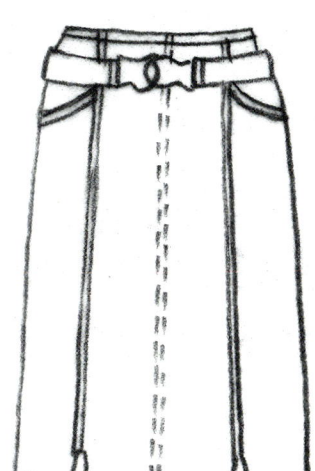

Variation of Skirts

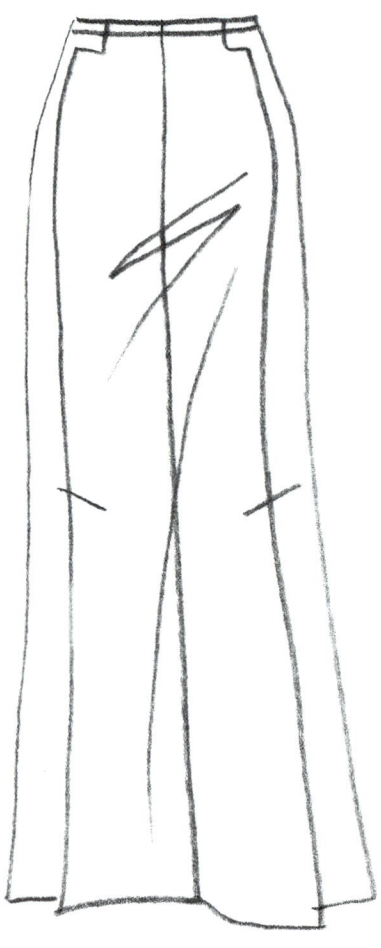
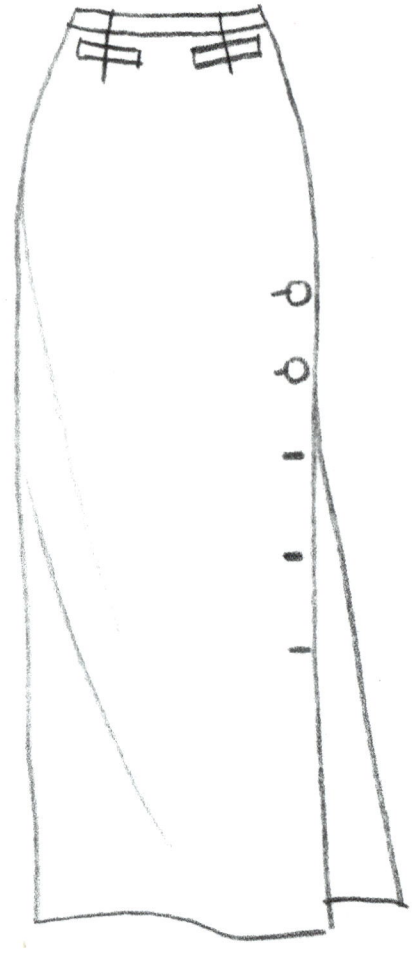
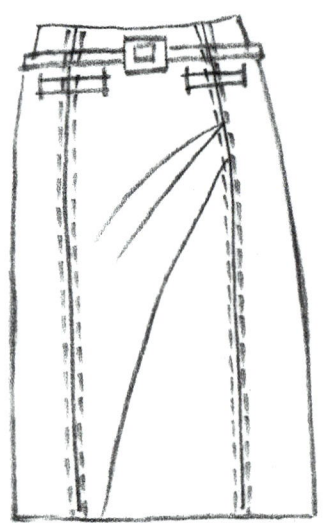
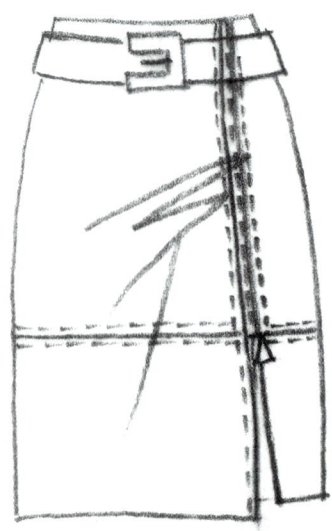

 Skirt

Variation of Skirts

Long Skirt

Short Skirt

25

 Skirt

Variation of Skirts

Variation of Skirts

Skirt

Variation of Skirts

Skirt

Variation of Skirts

Skirt

Variation of Skirts

Variation of Skirts

Tops

Variation of Tops

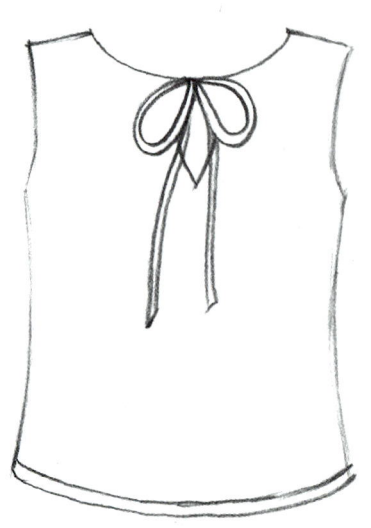

Tops

Variation of Tops

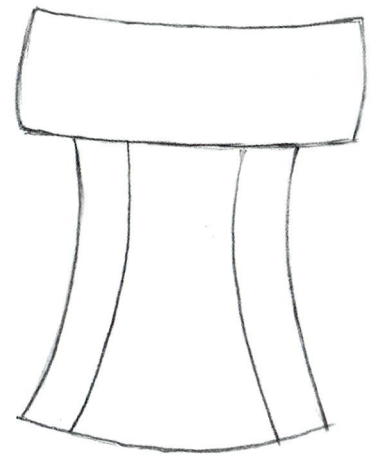
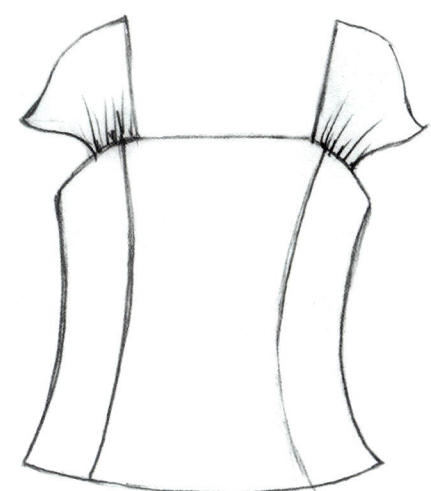
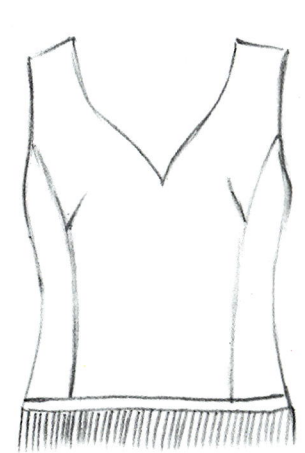

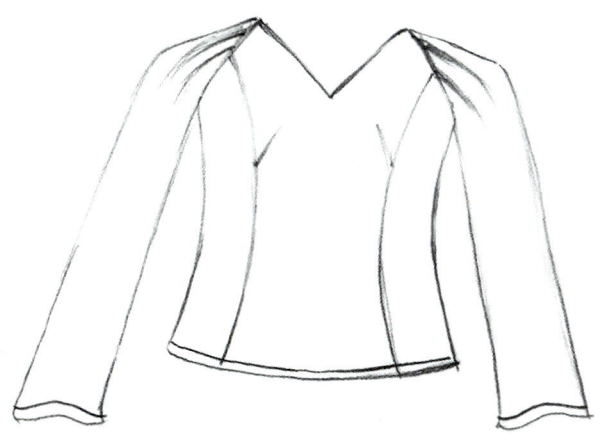

Tops

Variations of Skirts & Tops

Tops

Variation of Tops

Tops

Variation of Tops

Tops

Variation of Tops

Tops

Variation of Tops

38

Tops

Variation of Tops

Tops

Variation of Tops

40

Tops

Variation of Tops

41

Tops

Variation of Tops

Pants

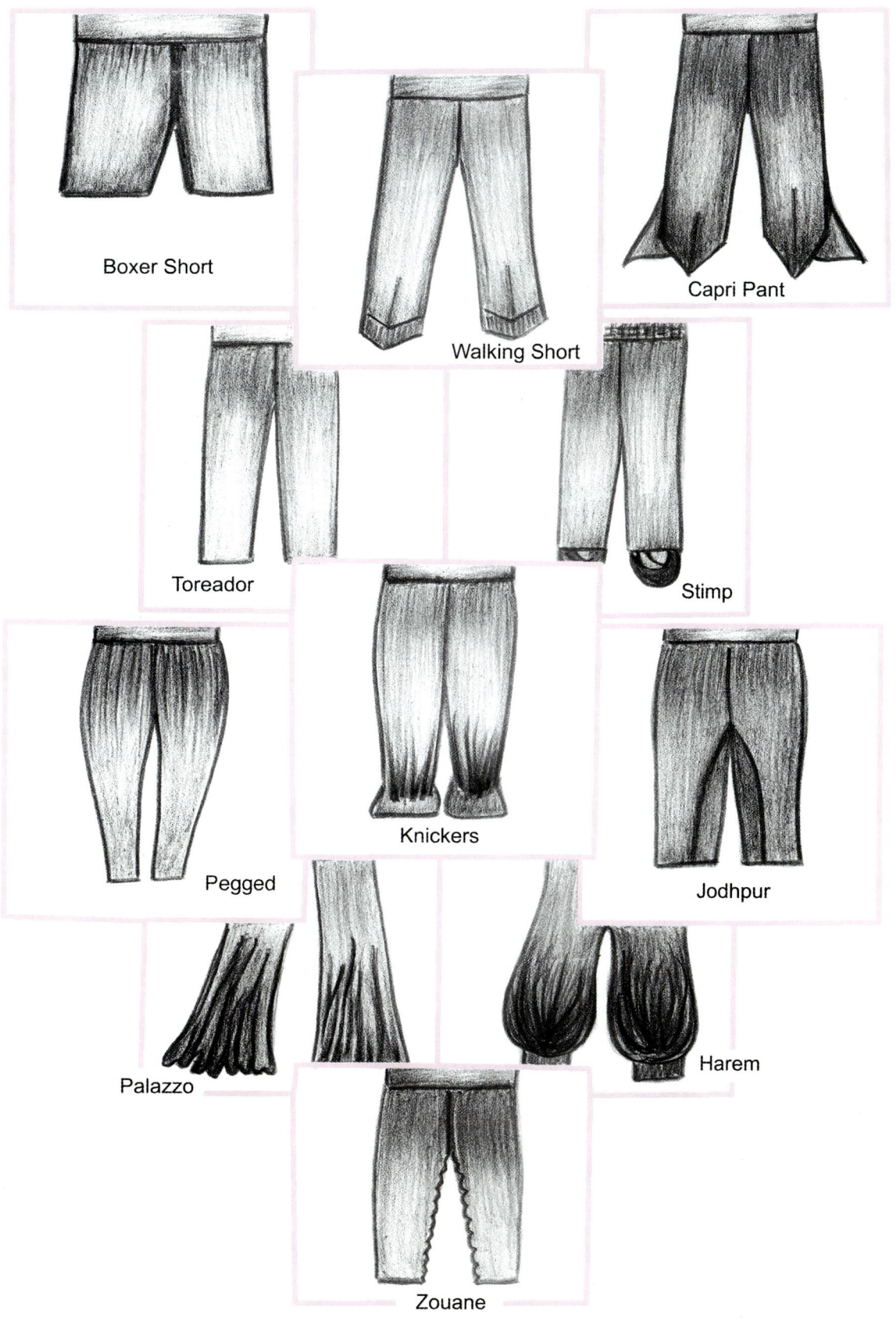

Pants

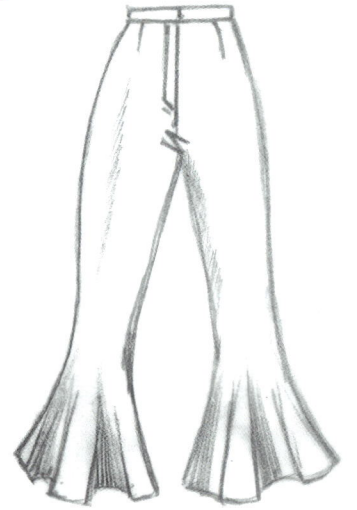
Bell Bottoms

Harem

Hot Pants with Bib

Palazzo

Short Skirt

loomers

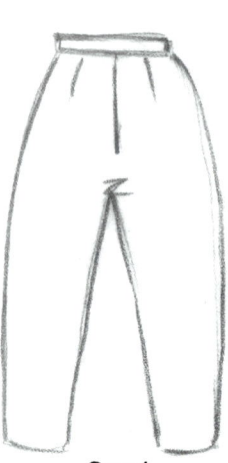
Capri

Pants

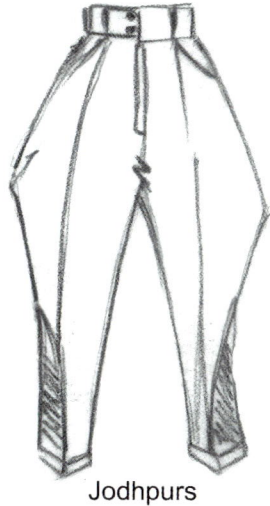
Jodhpurs

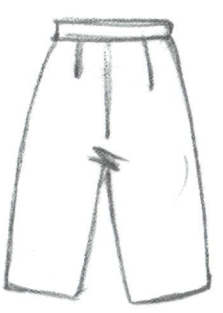
Bermudas

Ski Pants

Baggy Jeans

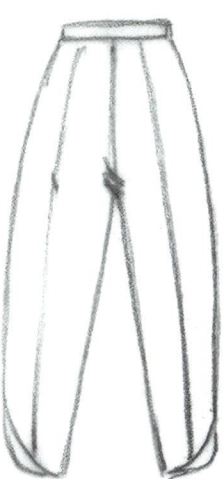
Toreador

Dungrees

Flares

Pants

Variations of Pants

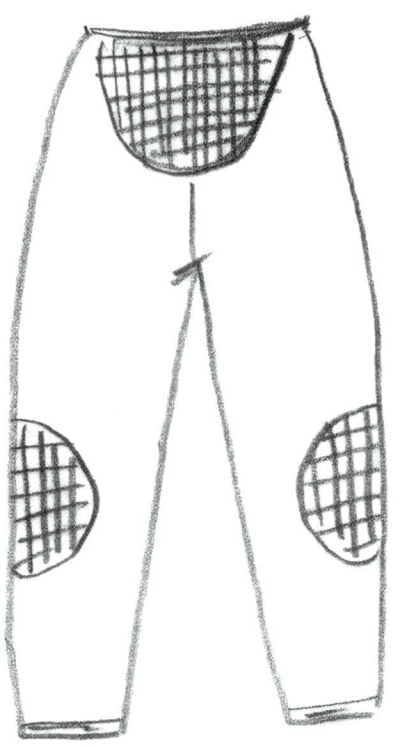

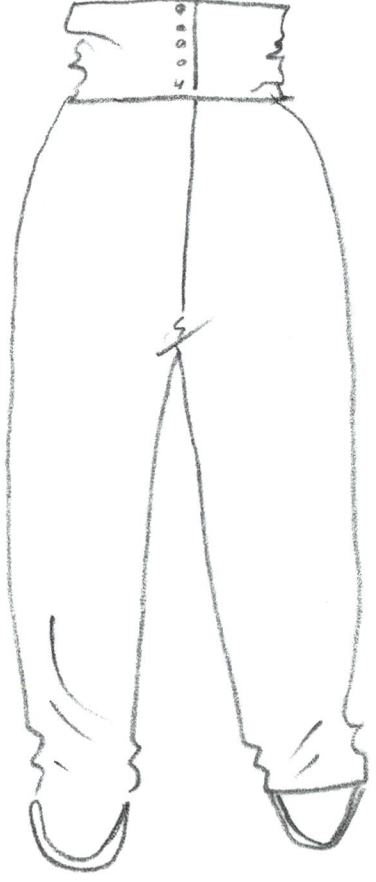

Variations of Pants

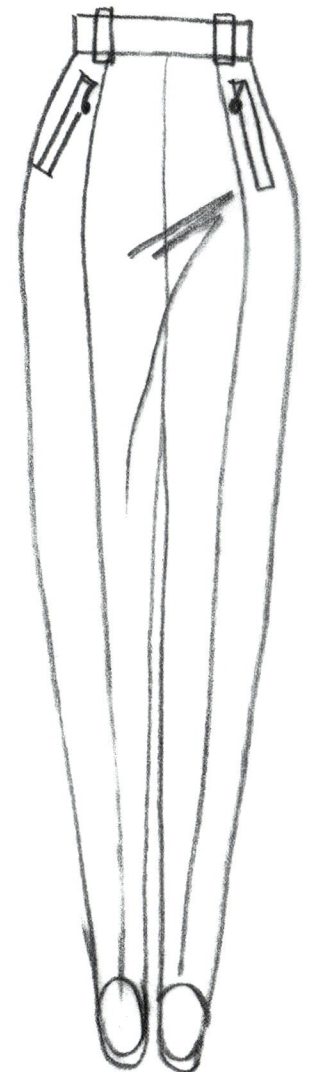
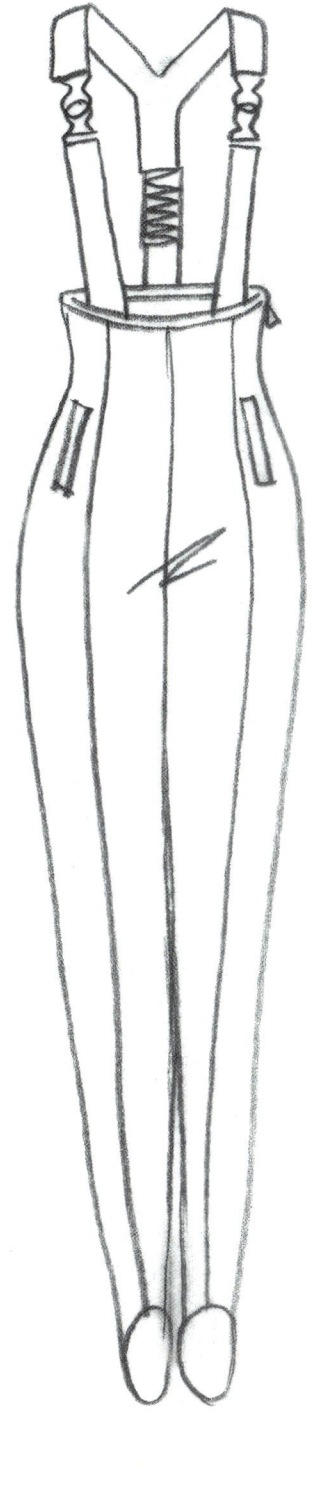
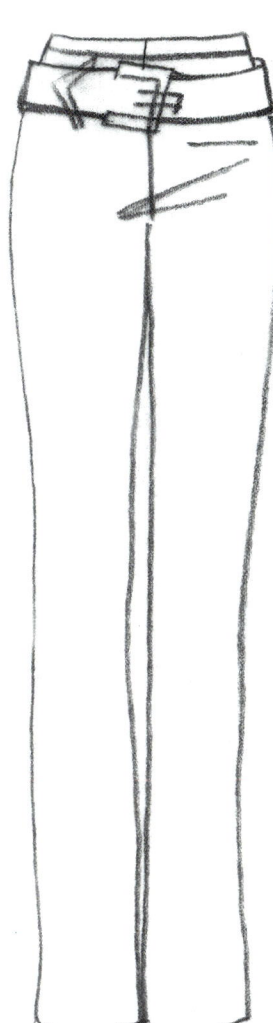

Pants

Variations of Pants

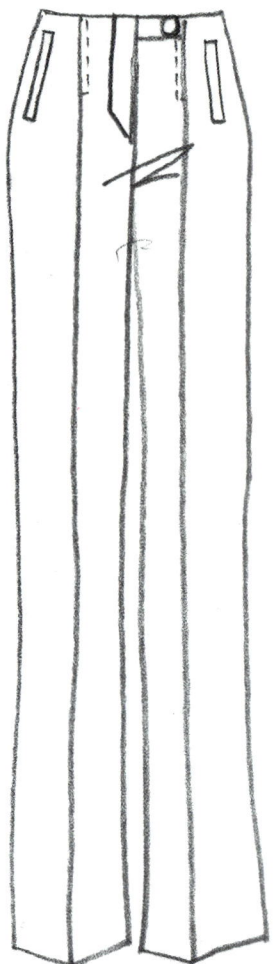
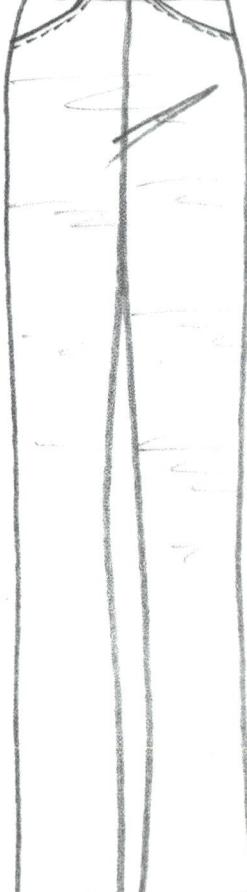
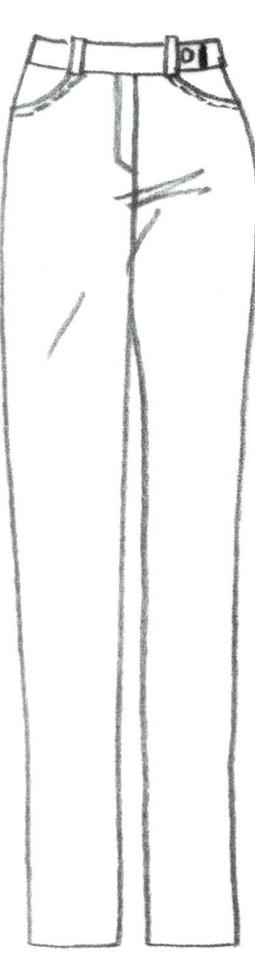

Pants

Variations of Pants

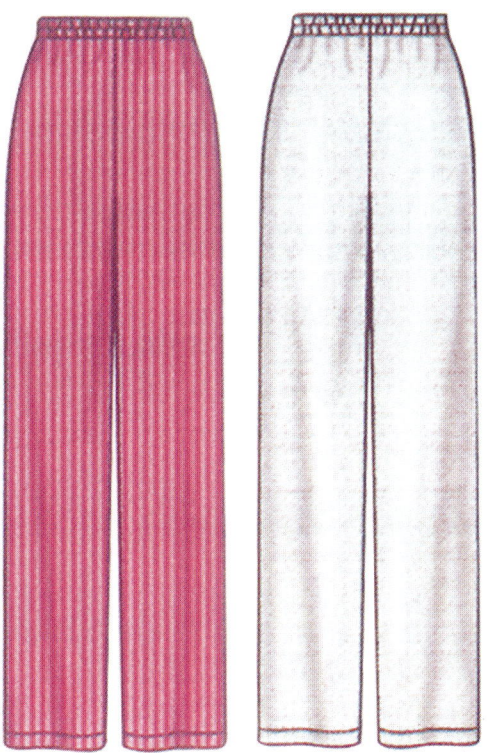

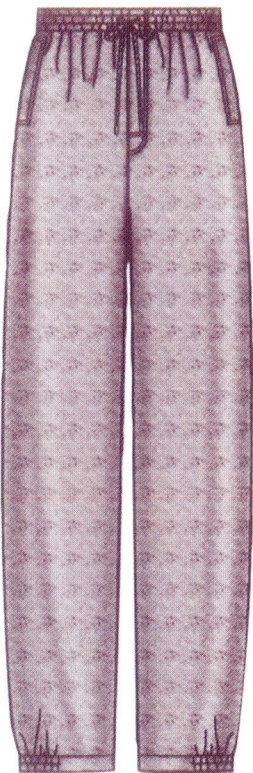

Pants

Variations of Pants

Pockets

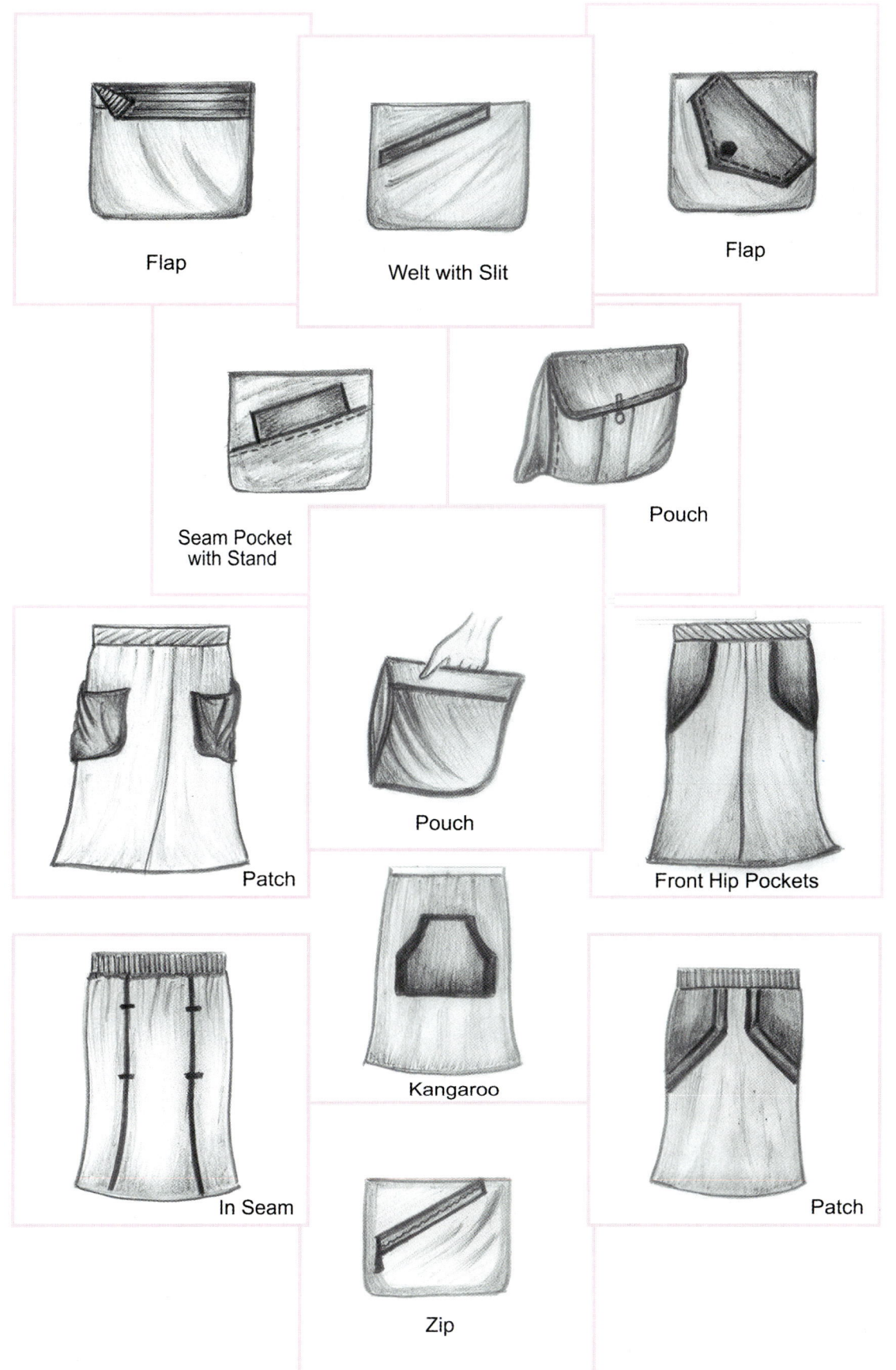

Pockets

Variations of Pockets

52

Tucks

Cross

Shell

Blind

Pin

Released

Yokes

| V-Yokes | Glass Yokes | Shoulder | Square |

Shirring

Frills & Flounces

Frills

Flounces

Frills & Flounces in Skirts

Bows & Drapes

Bows

Drapes

Jabot & Quilting

Jabot

Quilting

Fringing & Laces

Fringing

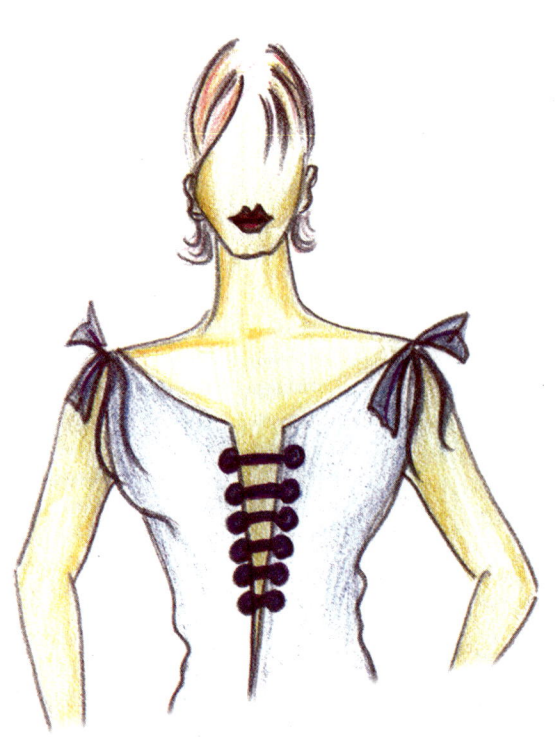

Laces

Kids wear

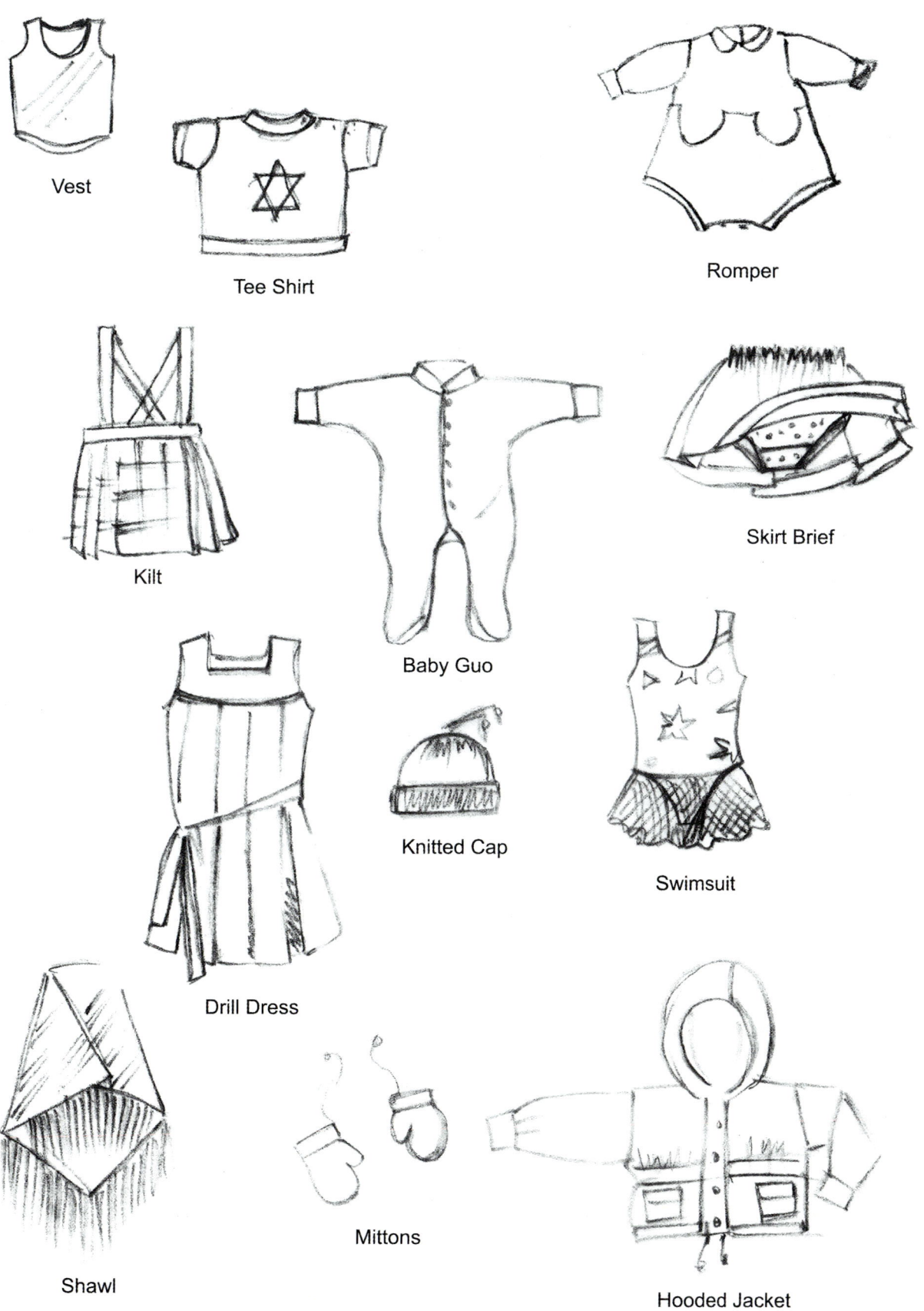

Kids wear

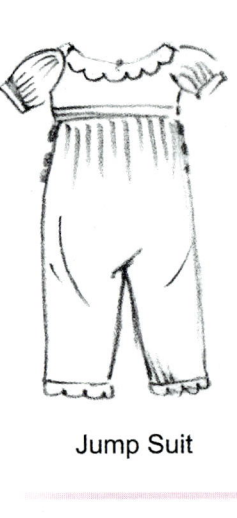
Jump Suit

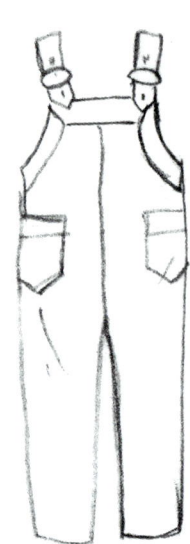
Brownie Suits

Jacket Suit

Sleeping Bag

Over Dress

Splash Suit

Bib

Layered Frock

Kids wear

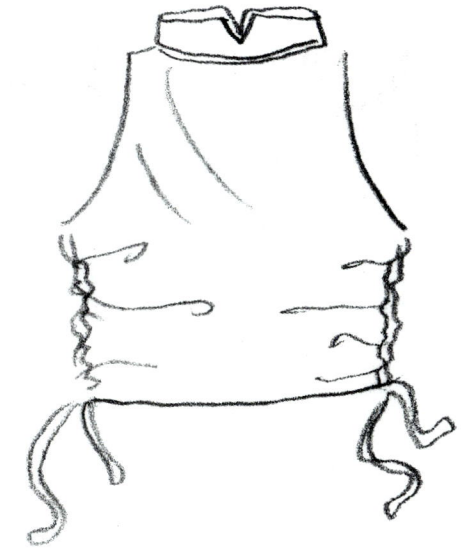

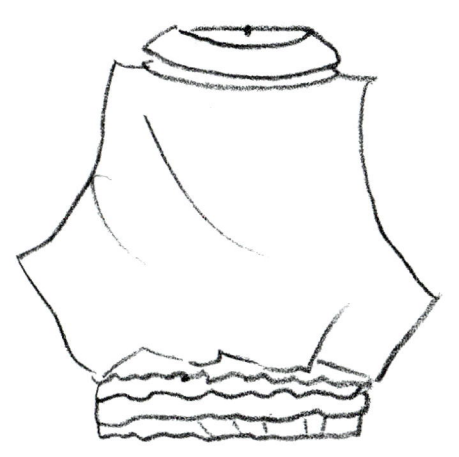
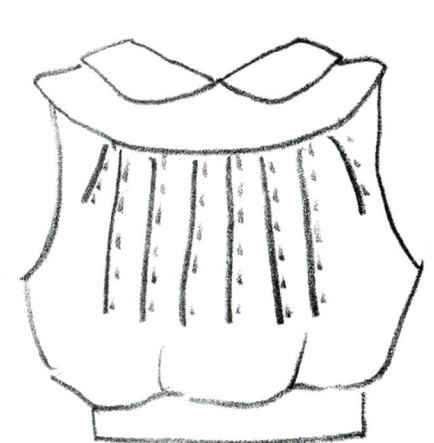

Kids wear

Kids wear

Kids wear

Variations of Jackets & Coats

Variation of Jackets

Variations of Jackets & Coats

Over Coats

Variations of Jackets & Coats

Over Coats

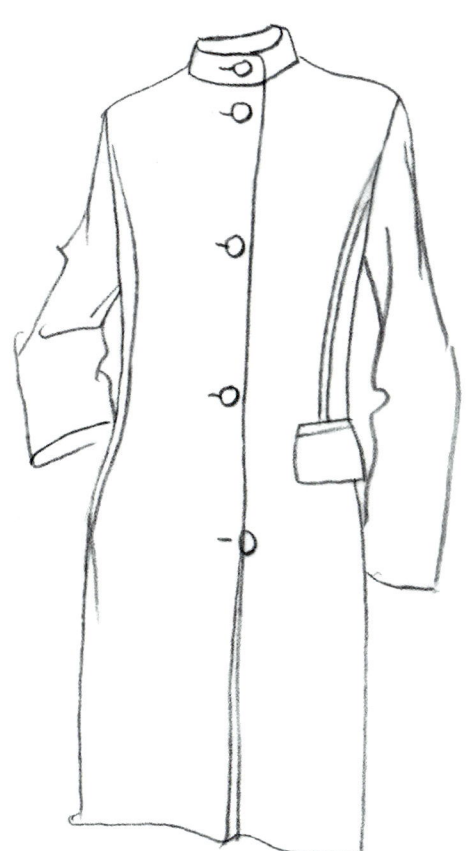

Variations of Jackets & Coats

Coats

Variations of Jackets & Coats

Coats

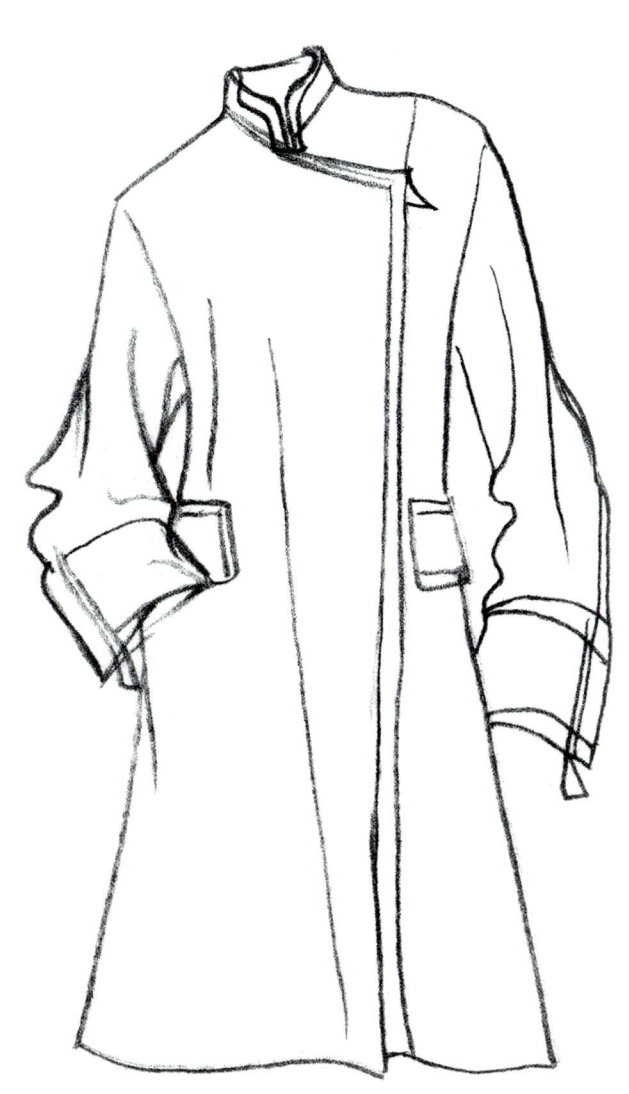

Variations of Jackets & Coats

Coats and Jacket

One piece dress

One piece dress

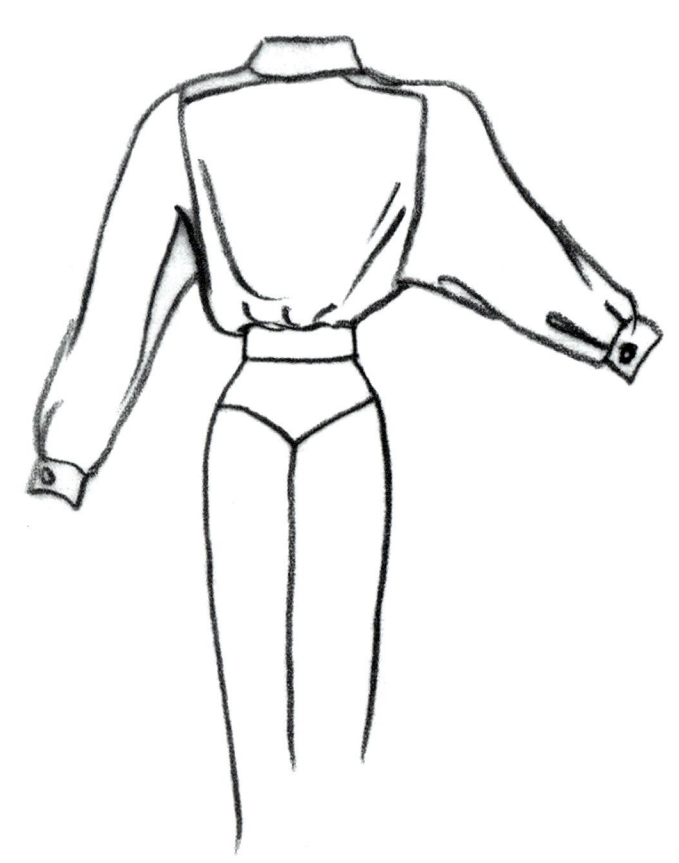

One piece dress

One piece dress

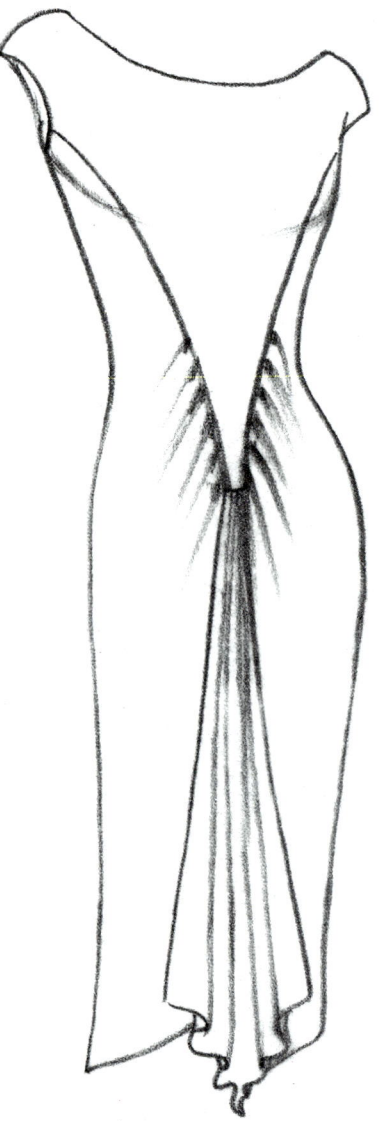

One piece dress

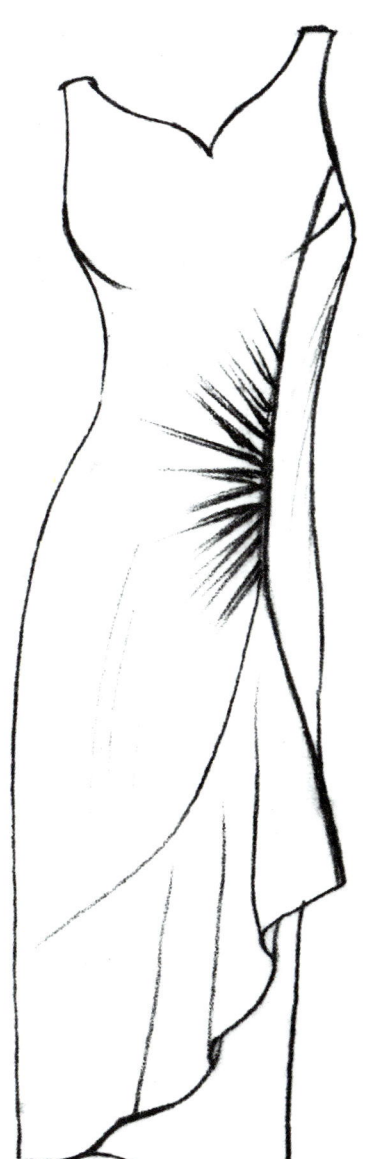
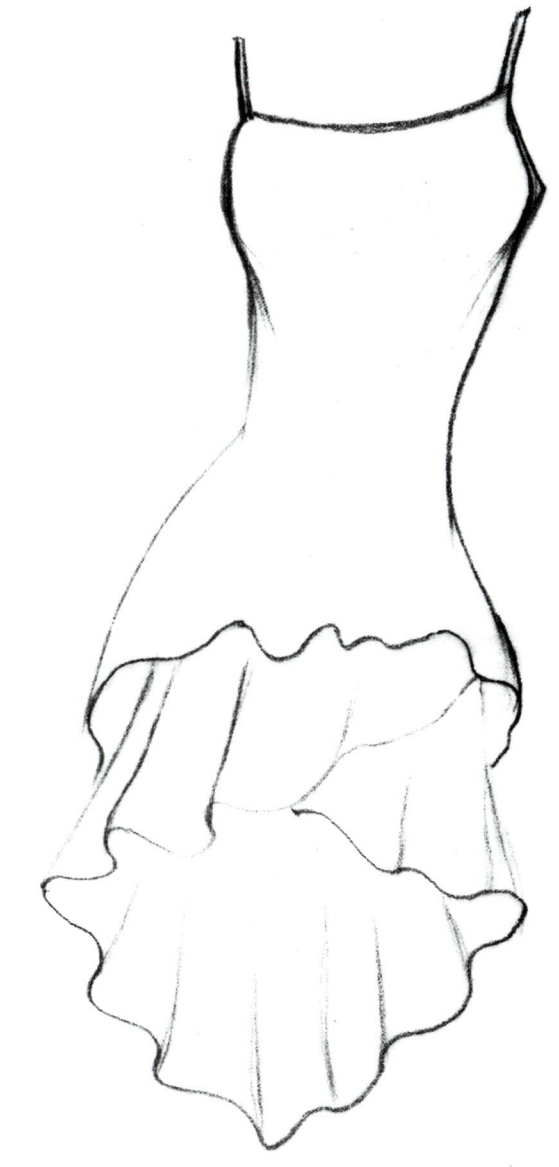

One piece dress

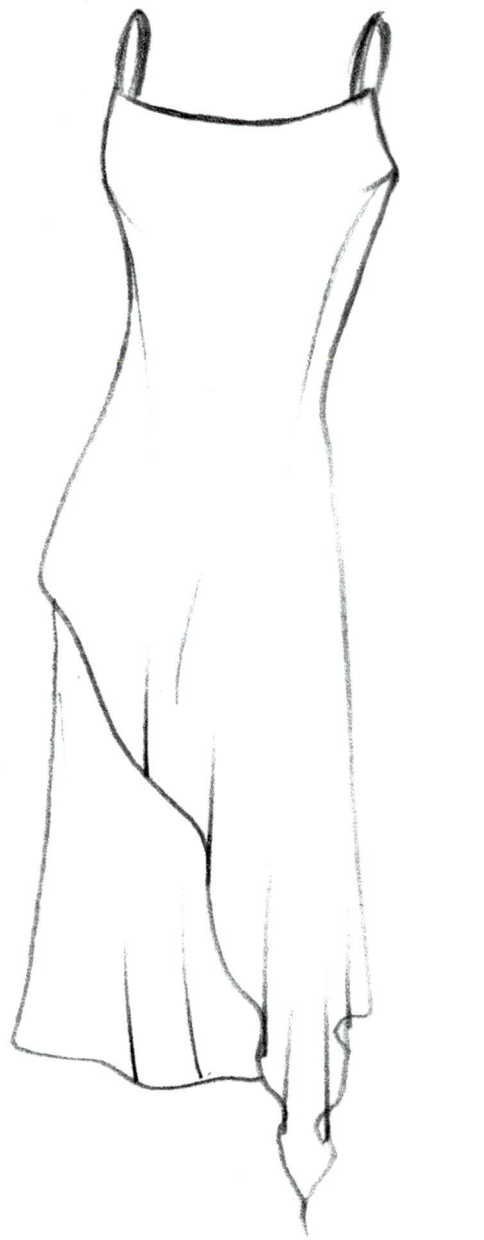
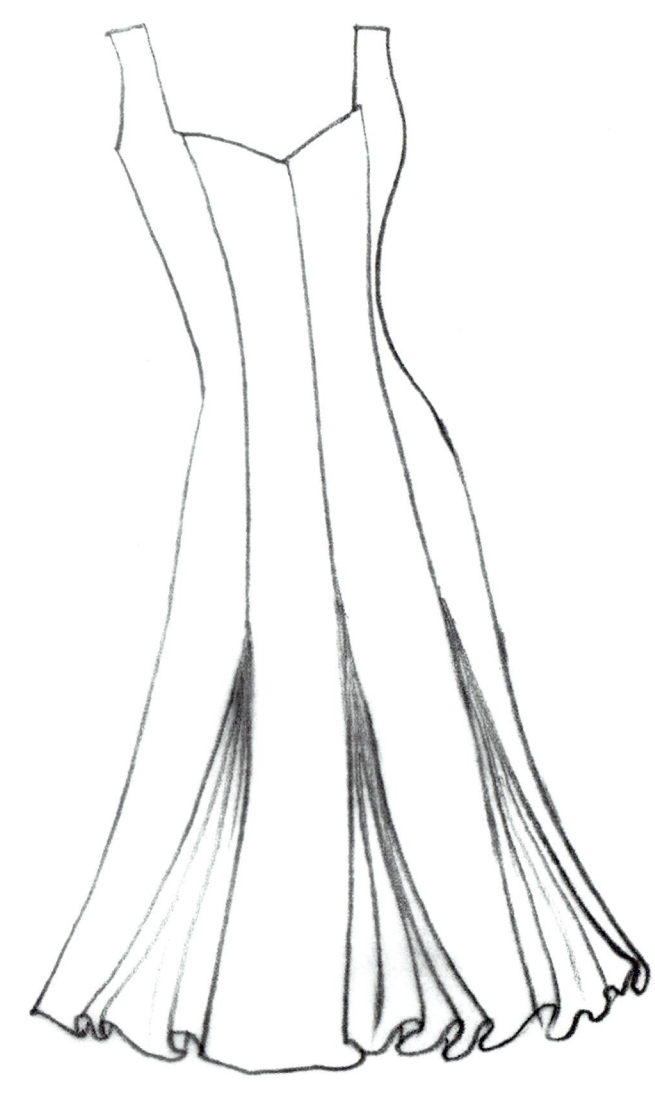

One piece dress

79

One piece dress

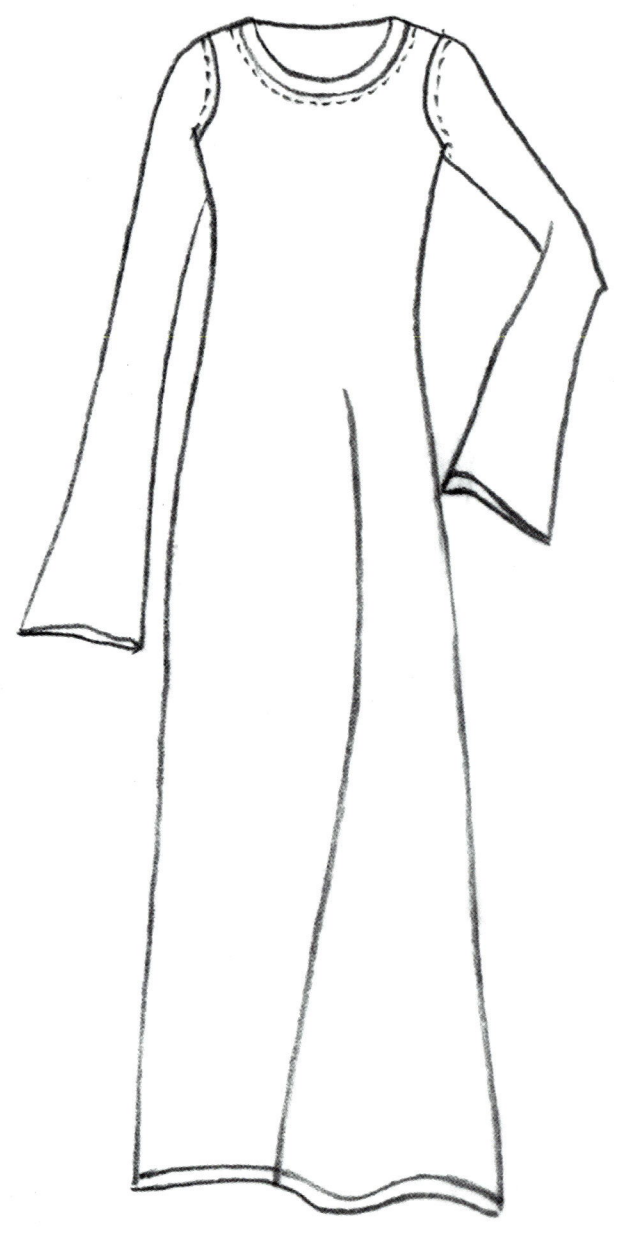

One piece dress

One piece dress

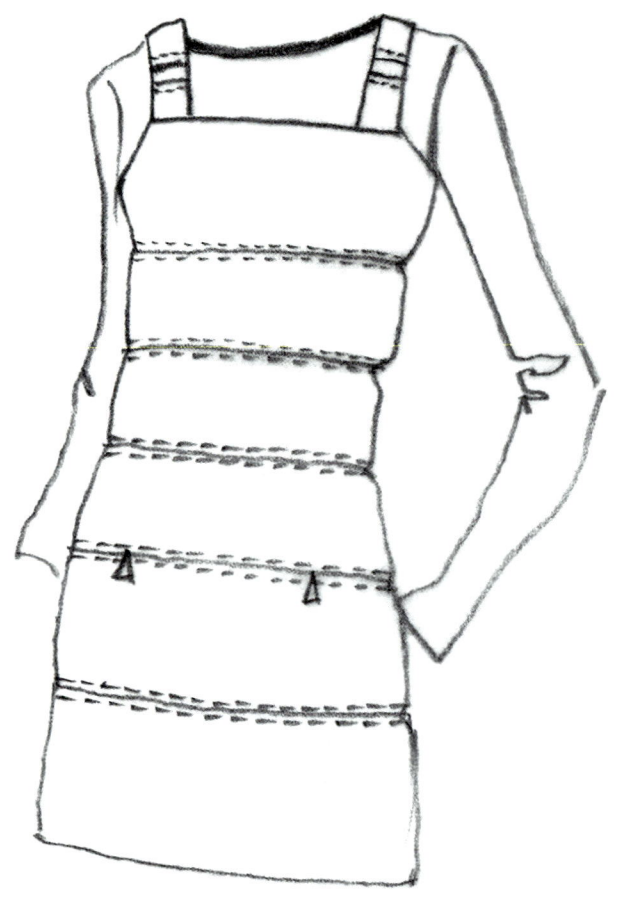

One piece dress

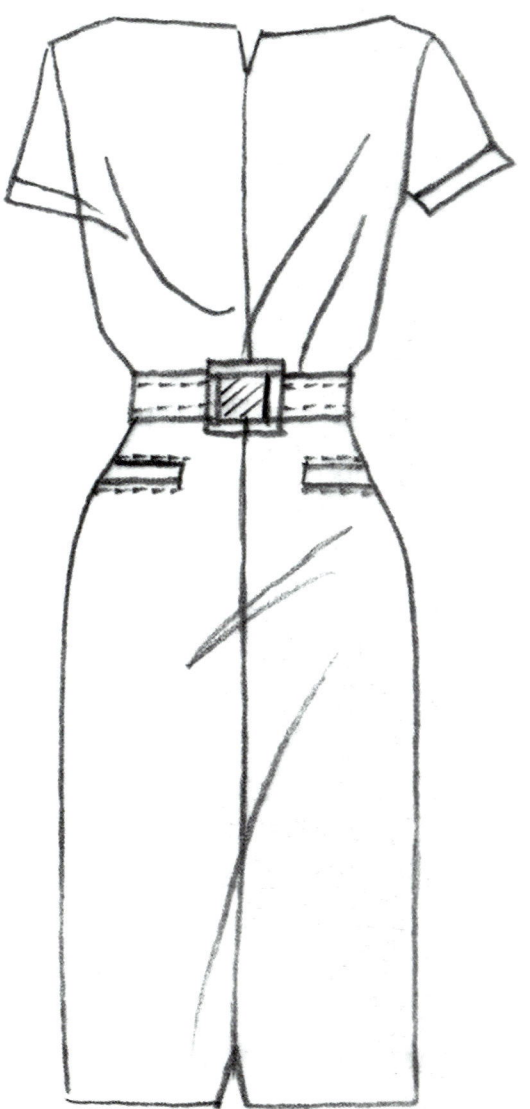

One piece dress

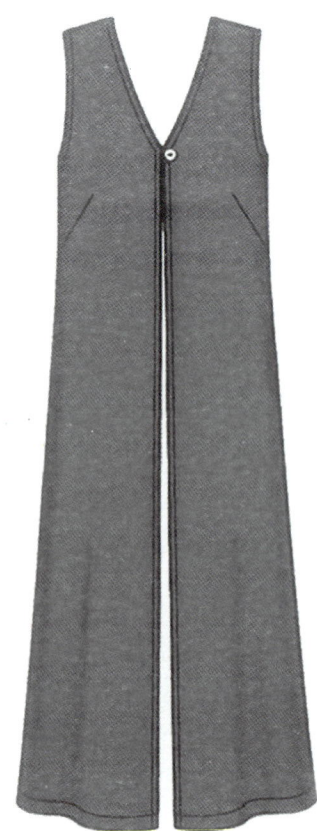

Variation of Frocks

 # Frock

Variation of Frocks

 # Frock

Variation of Frocks

Frock

Variation of Frocks

 # Frock

Variation of Frocks

 Frock

Variation of Frocks

Frock

Variation of Frocks

Jumpsuit

Jumpsuit

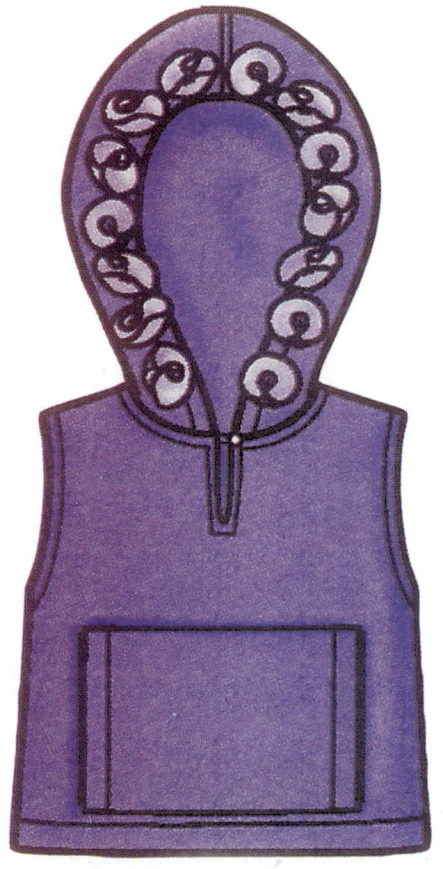

Jumpsuit

Poncho

Poncho

Dress

Dress

Dress

Dress

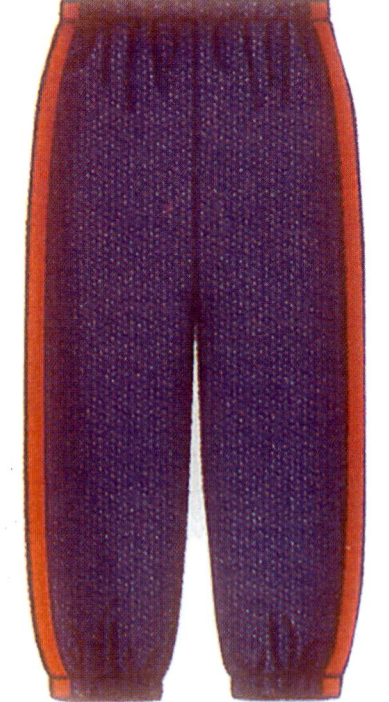

Dress

Dress

Dress

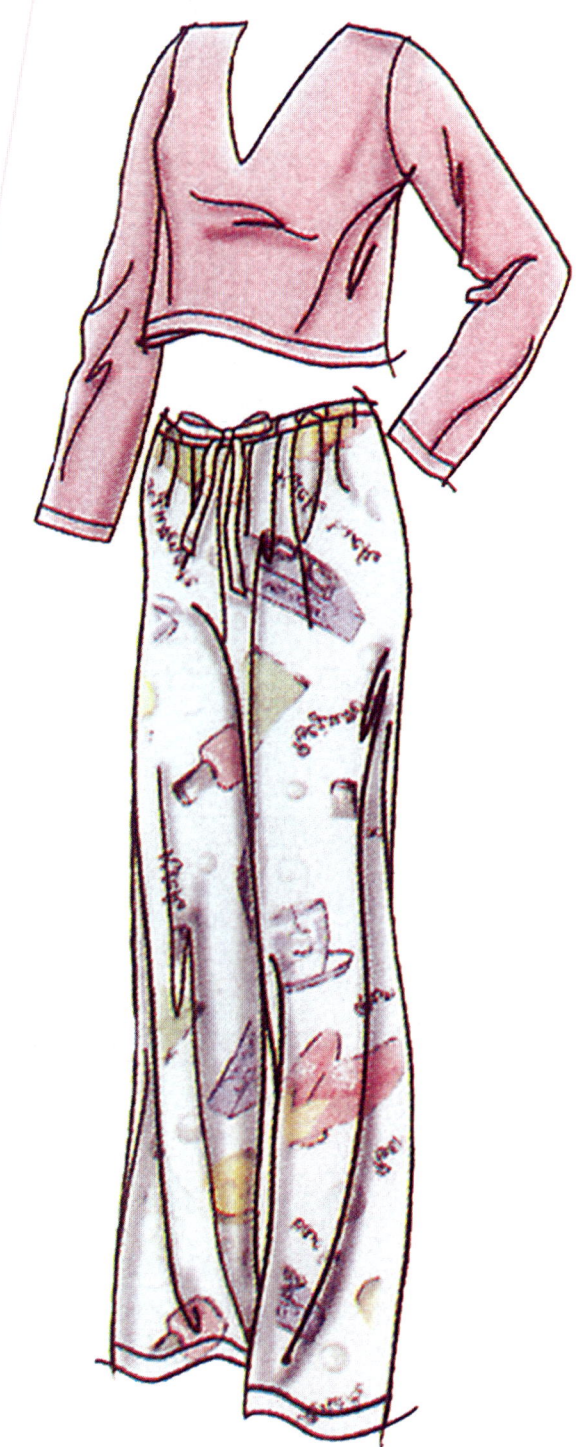

Dress

Dress

Dress

Dress

Jacket

108

Jacket

Nightwears

Nightwears

Nightwears

Nightwears

Loungewear

Loungewear

Loungewear

Loungewear

Loungewear

Loungewear

*L*oungewear

Nature Study

Object drawing

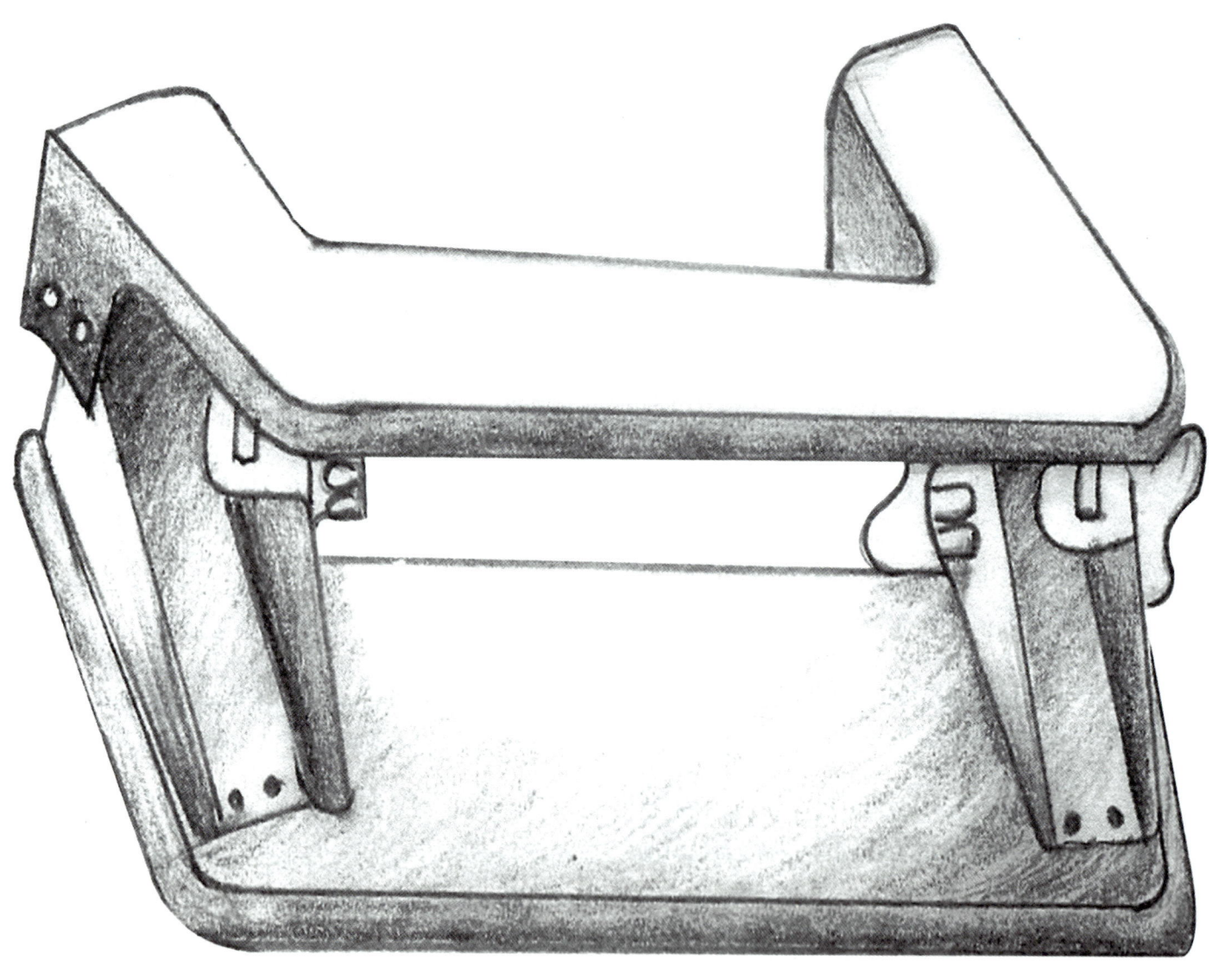

Object drawing

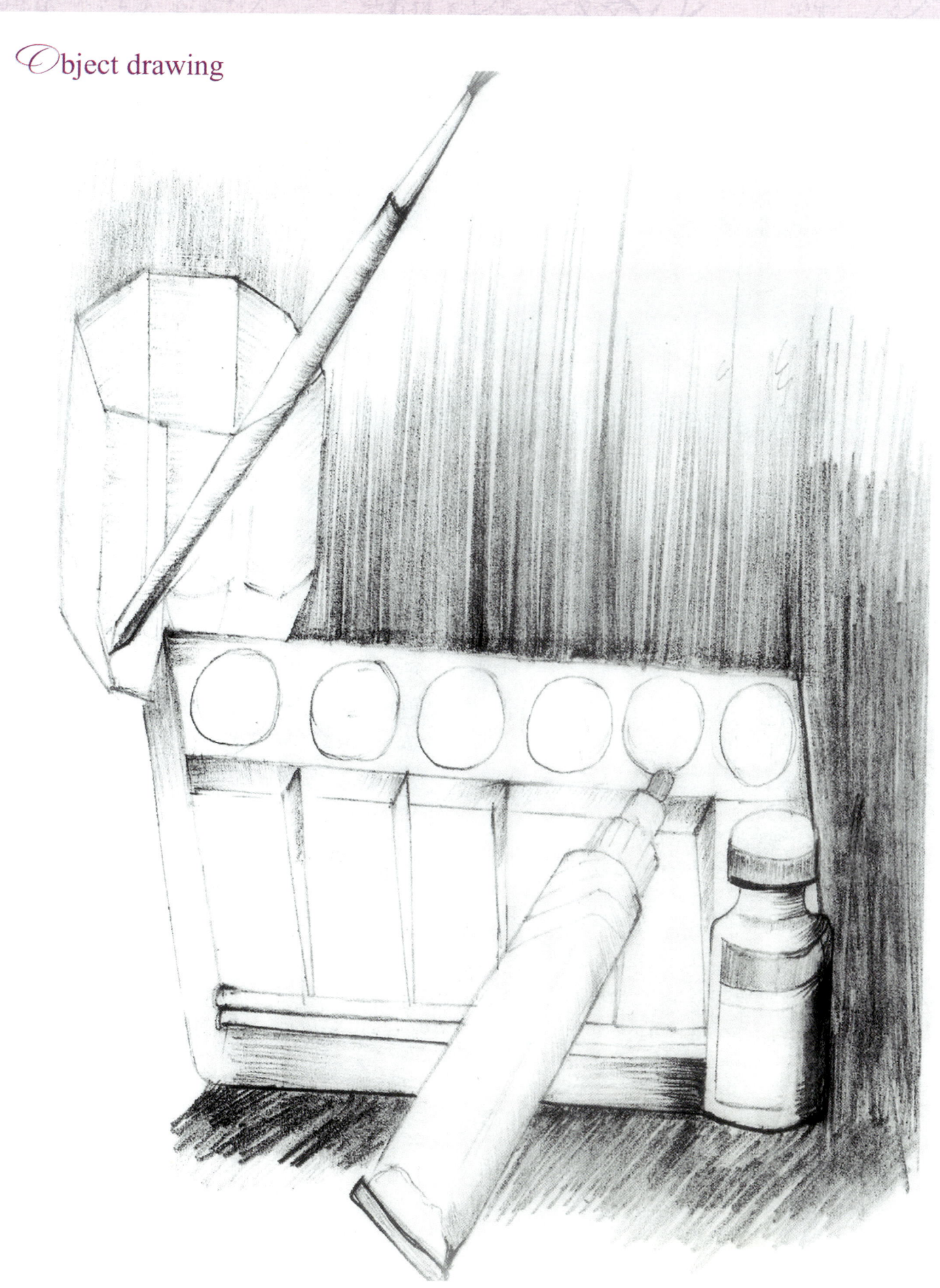

Object drawing

Object drawing

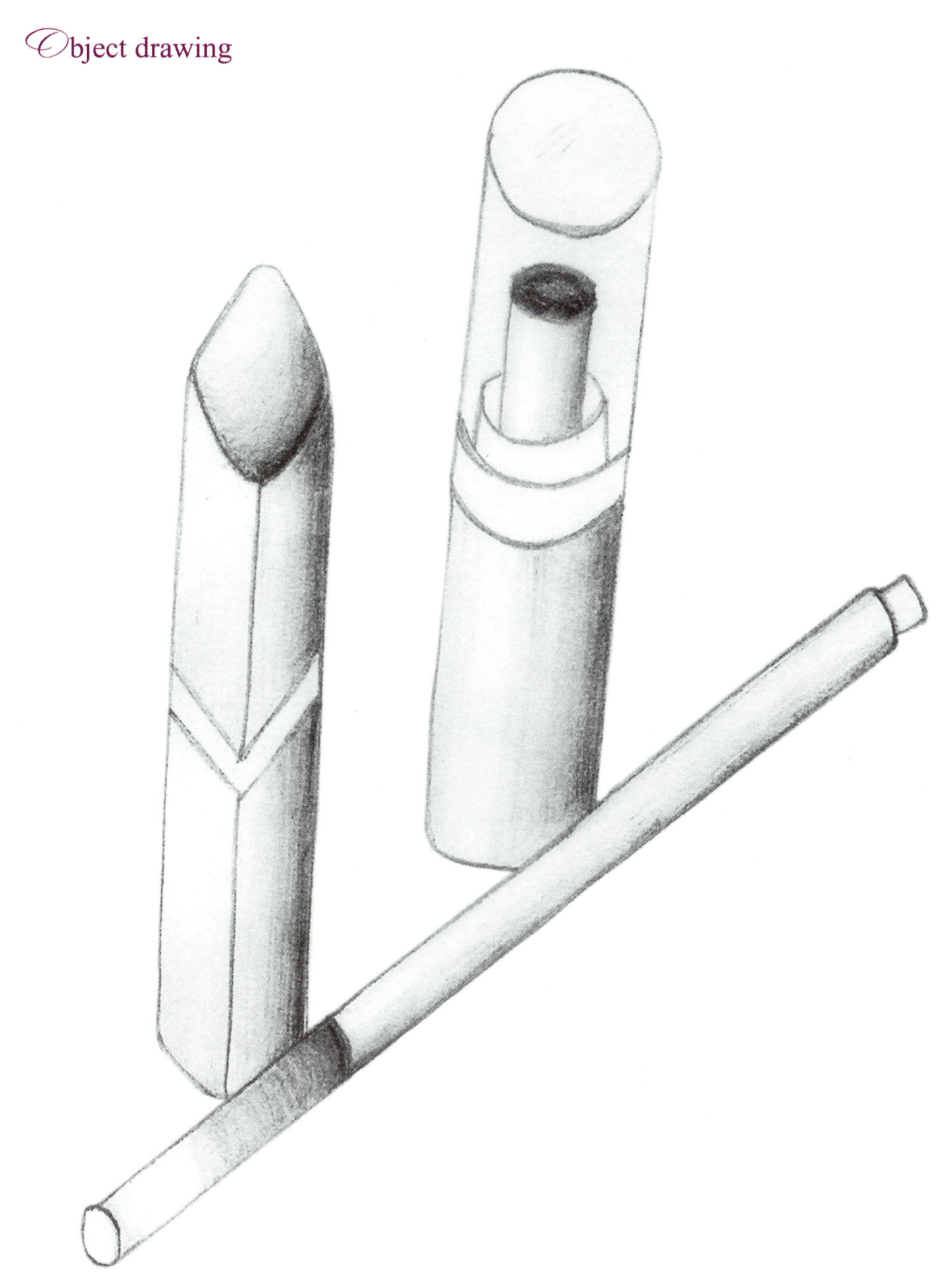

Object drawing

Object drawing

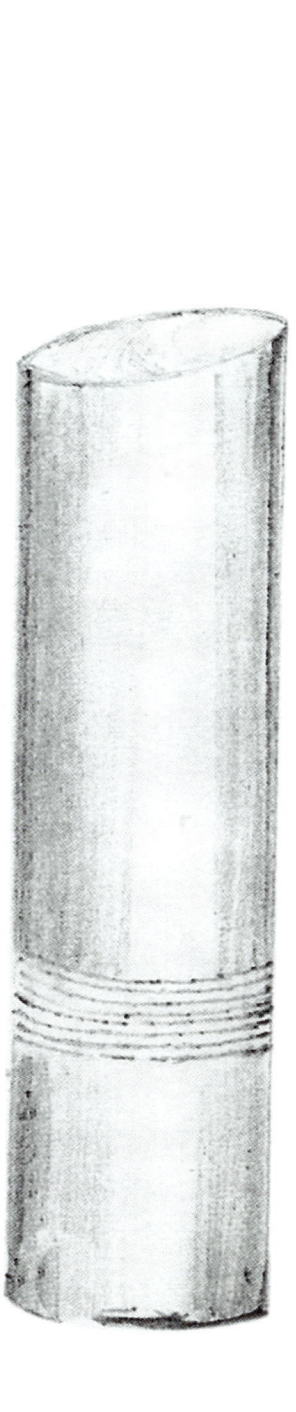

Object drawing

Object drawing

Shoes

Shoes

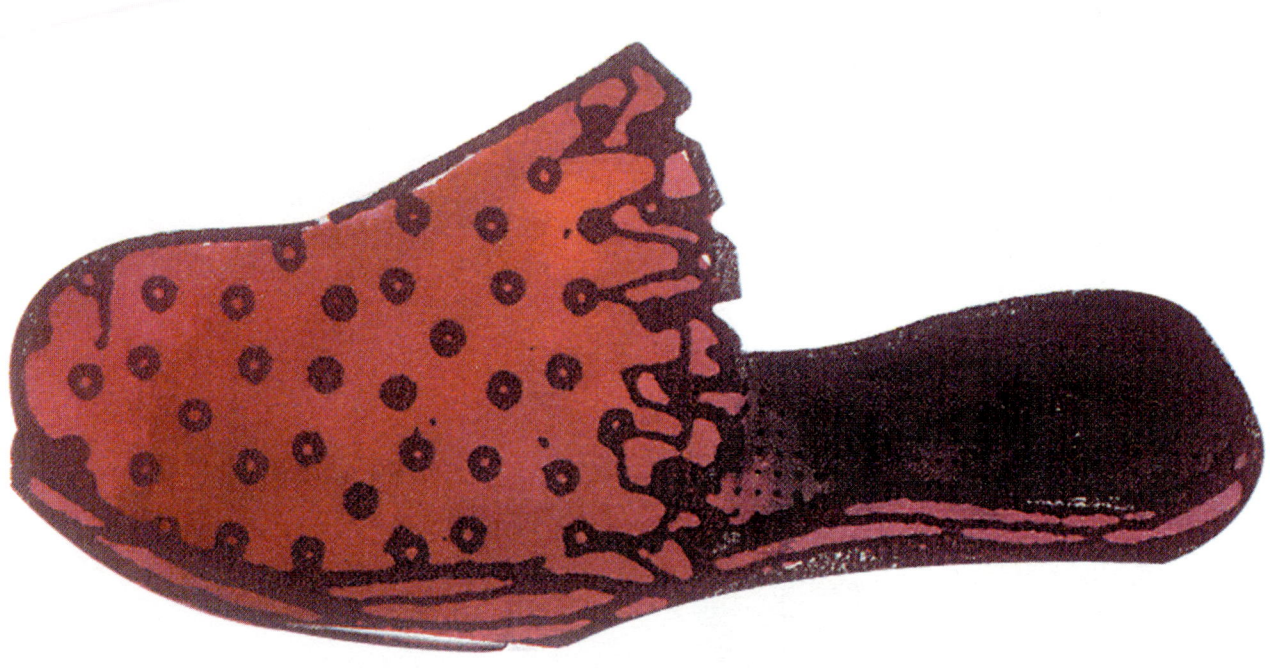

Shoes

Bag's

Bag's

Bag's

Bag's

Bag's

Neck accessories

Neck accessories

Belts

Belts

Belts

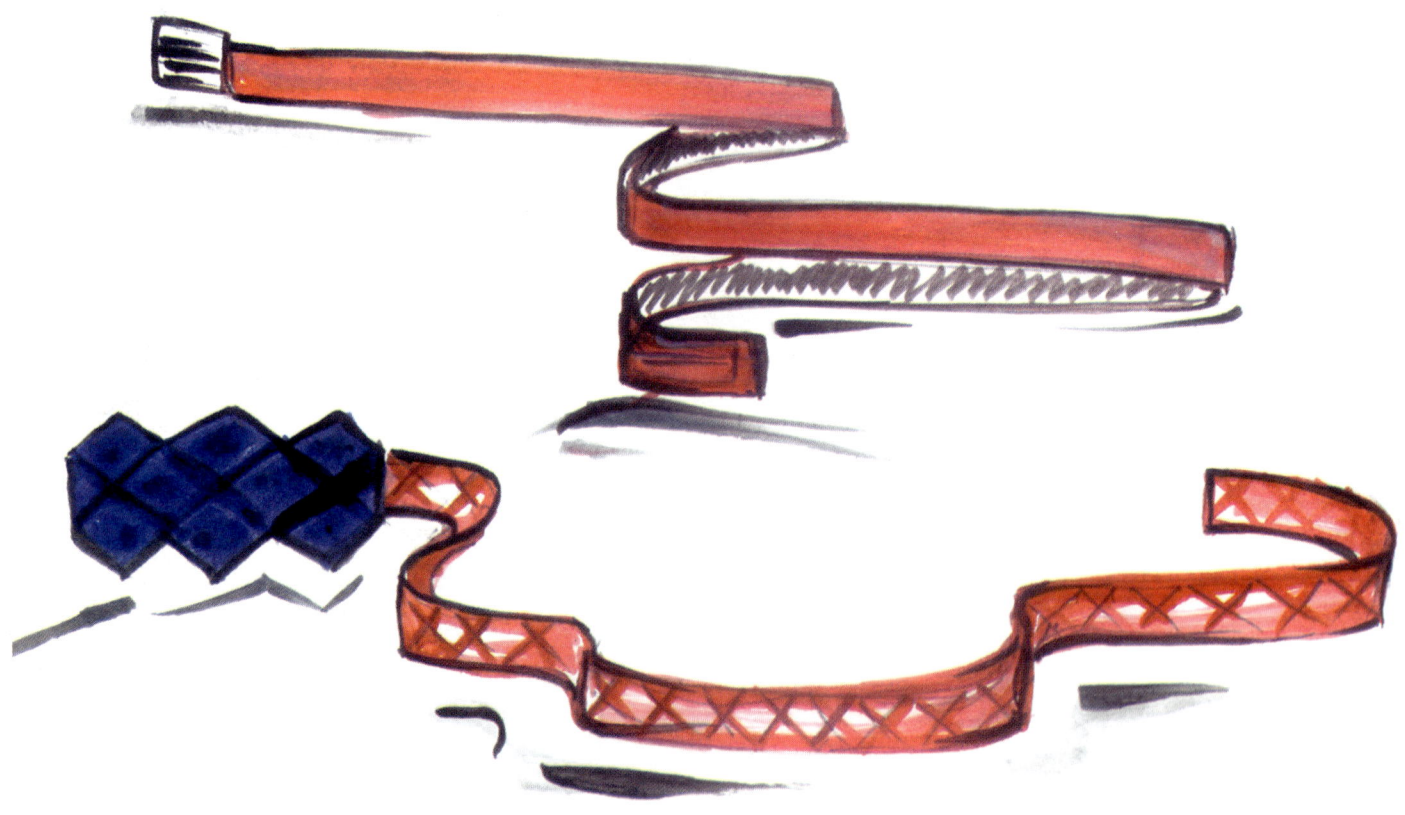

Composition

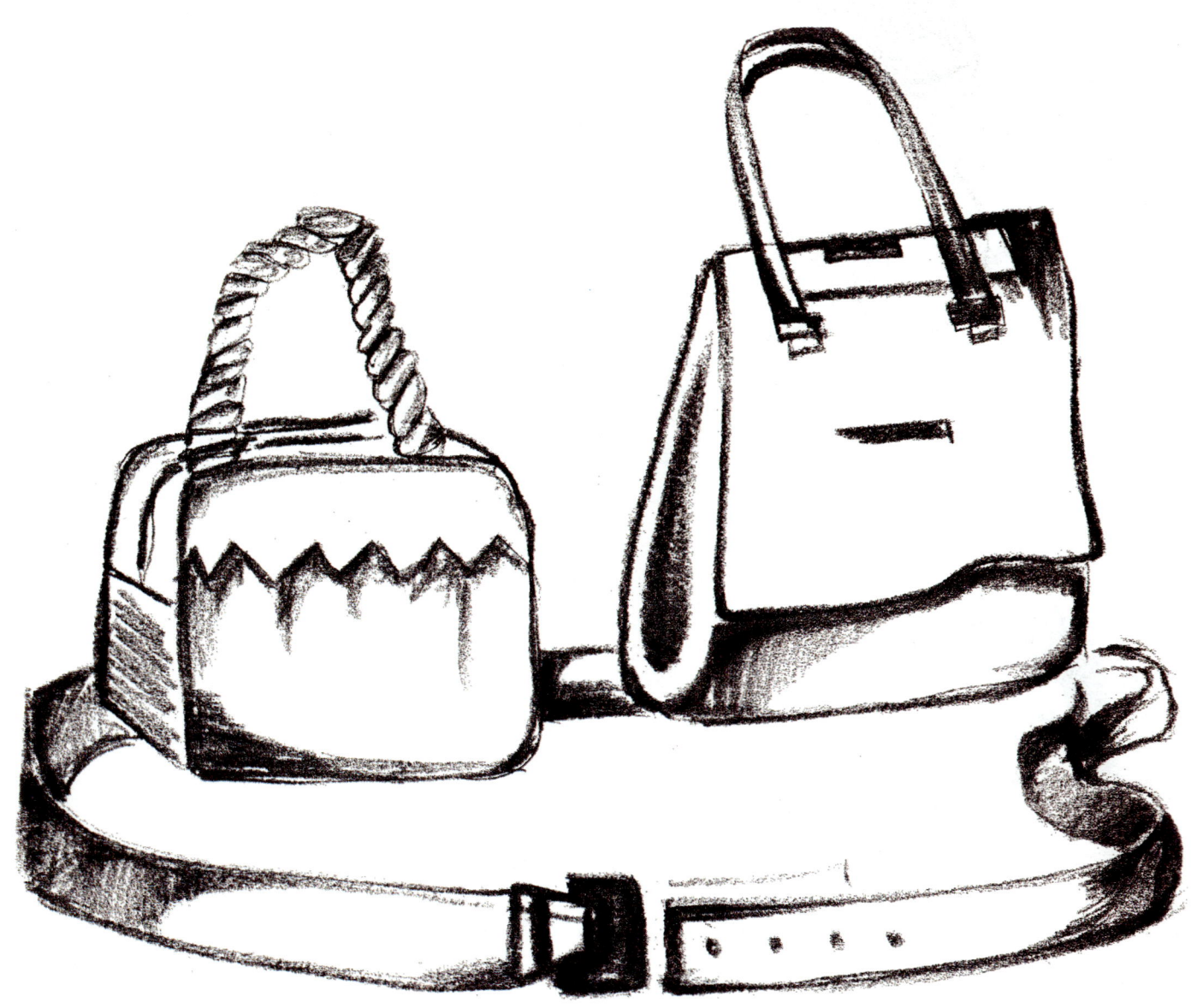

Composition

Composition

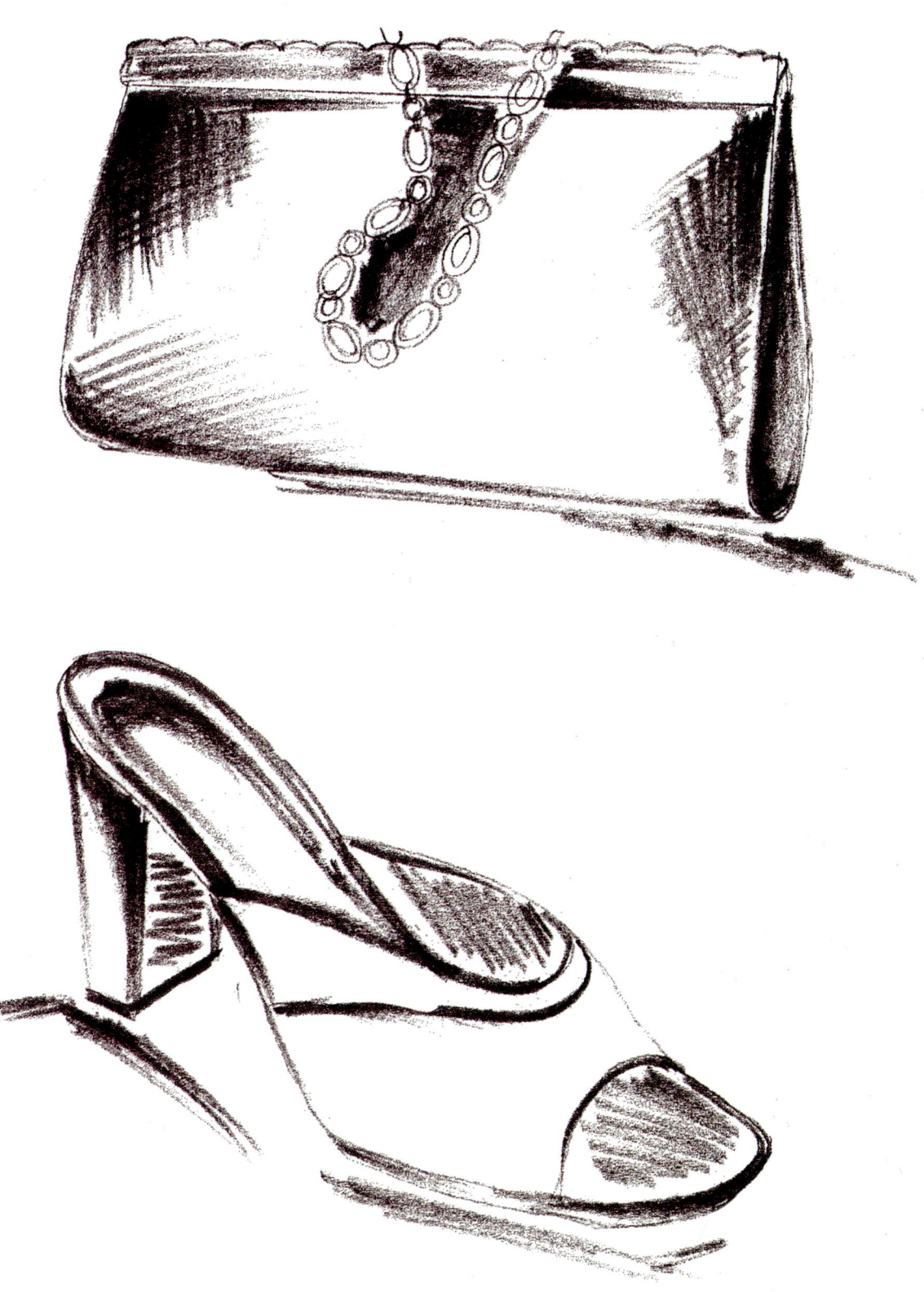

Composition

Composition

Composition

Composition

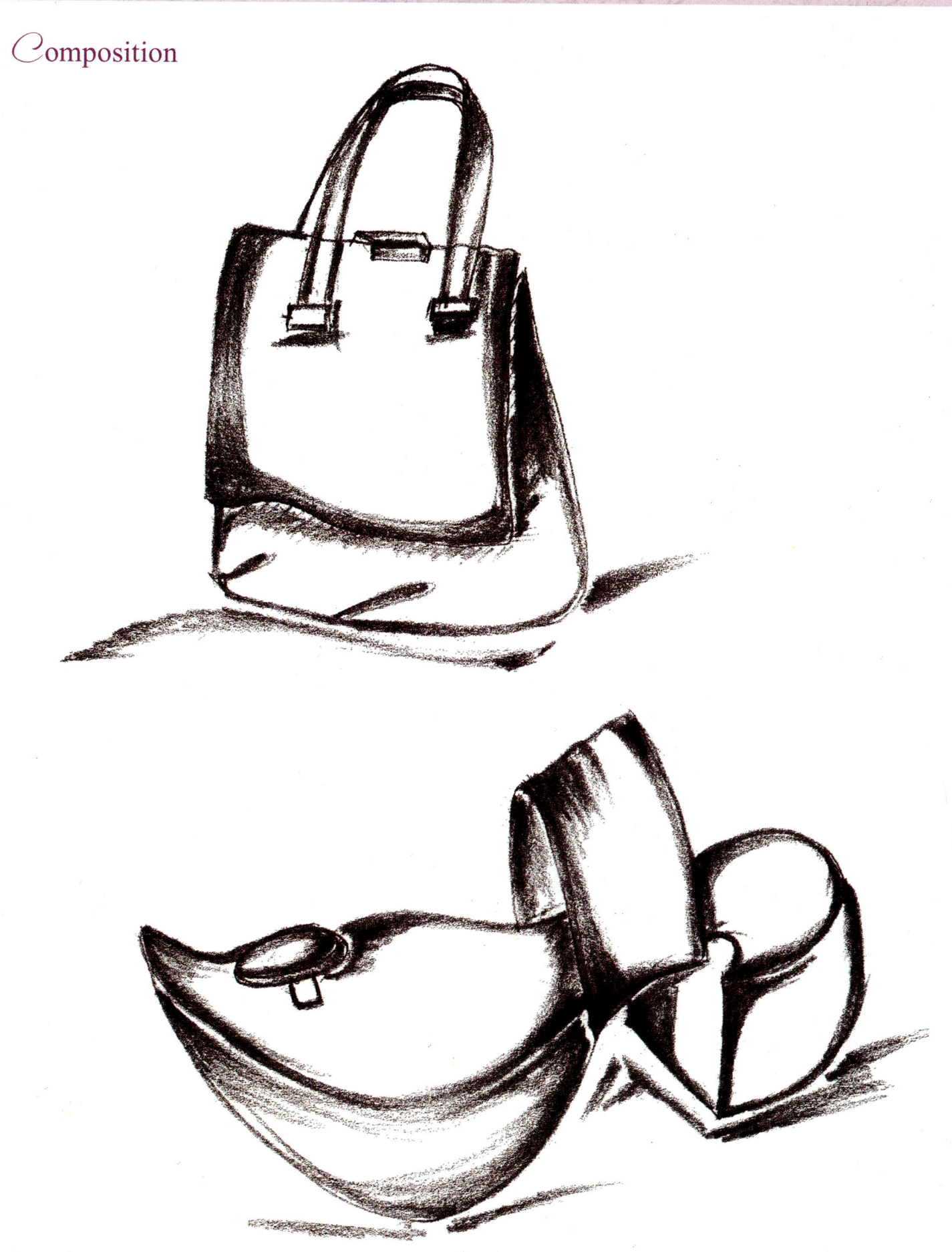

Composition

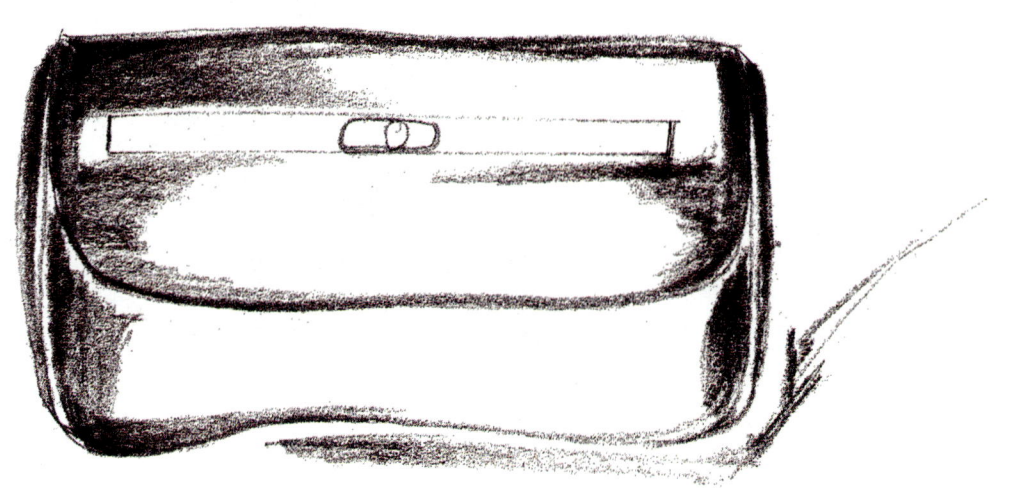

Composition

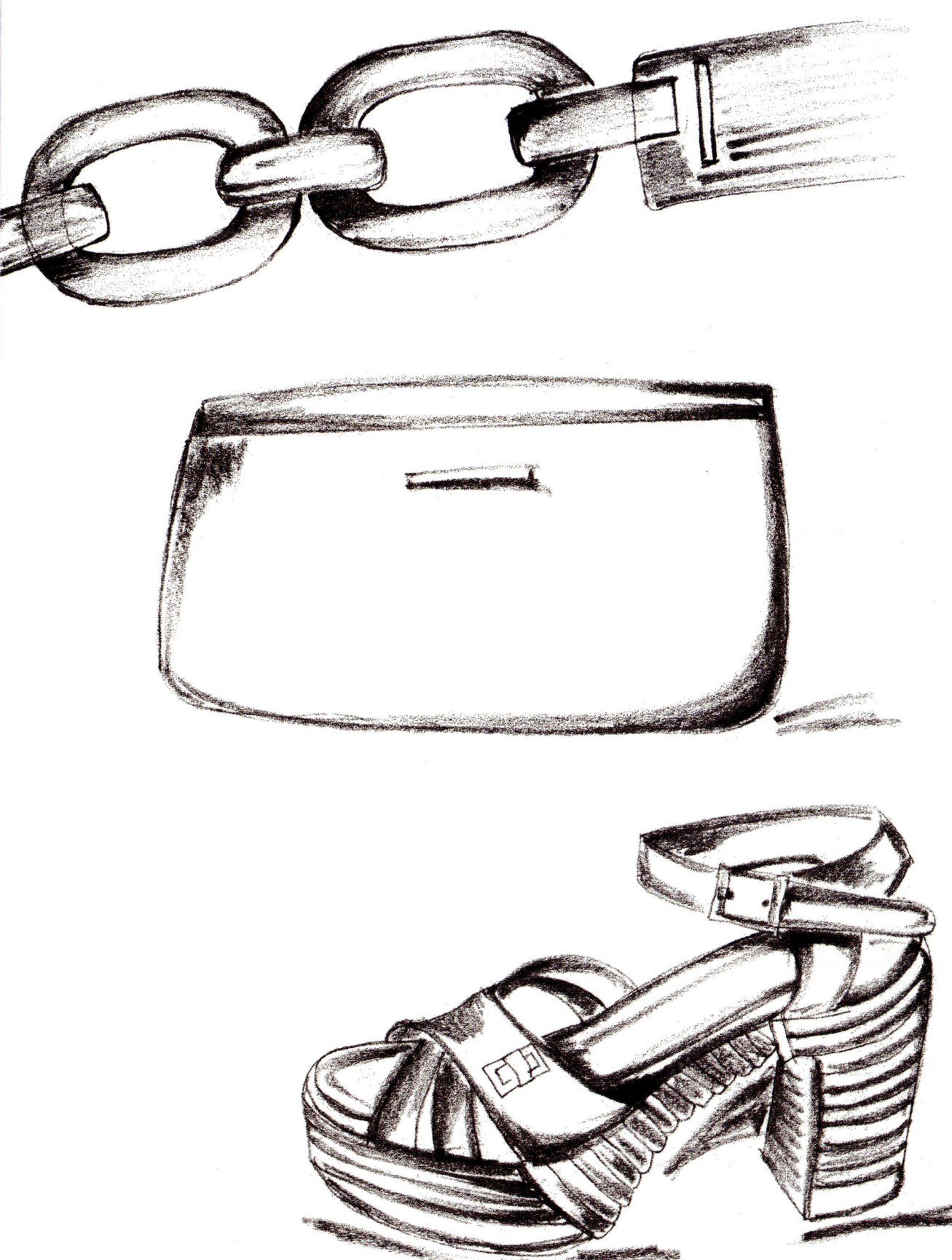

Composition

Composition

Composition

Composition

Composition

Composition

Composition

Composition

Composition

Composition

Composition

Composition

Hats

Variation of Hats

ats

Variation of Hats